INDIAN VEGETARIAN COOKING FROM AN AMERICAN KITCHEN

RANDOM HOUSE NEW YORK

INDIAN VEGETARIAN COOKING FROM AN AMERICAN KITCHEN

VASANTHA PRASAD

LIBRARY OF CONGRESS CATALOGING-IN-PUBLICATION DATA
Prasad, Vasantha.
Indian vegetarian cooking from an American kitchen /
Vasantha Prasad
p.   cm.
ISBN 978-0-679-76438-0
1. Vegetarian cookery.   2. Cookery, India.   I. Title.
TX837.P73   1998   641.5'636—DC20   95-21501

Random House website address: www.randomhouse.com

146712470

TO MY LOVING PARENTS,

ESPECIALLY MY MOTHER,

WHO INSPIRED ME

TO LEARN AND ENJOY

THE FINE ART

OF INDIAN CUISINE

ACKNOWLEDGMENTS

*I am grateful to my wonderful husband, Balasa,
and my adorable daughter, Bindu. Their passion
for good vegetarian food motivated me to write
this book. Their continued support, encourage-
ment, and cooperation made this possible.*

*I always dreamed of introducing people to
healthy eating. Random House turned my dream
into a reality by publishing this book. I thank
them from the bottom of my heart. I also want
to thank Susan DiSesa, Beth Thomas, and
Dennis Ambrose for their enthusiasm, guidance,
and patient editing.*

*Last, I want to thank Emma C. Gardner and
Jennifer Eisenpresser, who illustrated and
designed this lovely book cover.*

CONTENTS

CONTENTS

INTRODUCTION

When I was a little girl in Bangalore, in southern India, I loved sitting on our kitchen counter every day after school and watching my *amma* (mother) cook. Balancing several pots on the stove, chopping vegetables, blending spices, she made everything look so easy and graceful. I was absolutely fascinated! When I asked her what makes her cooking so delicious, she answered that the secret ingredient to any meal is love.

Because refrigerators were not yet available in India, my mother would shop for fresh vegetables every day. Often I would accompany her, and on those trips she would teach me about selecting fruit and vegetables, relying on our senses to determine freshness. How does it look? she would ask. How does it smell? How does it feel in your hand? Every trip to the farmer's market to buy flowers, fruits, and vegetables was an adventure with her. Each neighborhood had a market, and you could smell its intoxicating scent from afar. Each vendor had a small cubicle averaging eight feet by ten feet and would either specialize by selling only one item such as bananas or coconuts or would sell a wide variety such as apples, apricots, cherries, guava, mangoes, melon, papaya, peaches, pears, pomegranates, and tomatoes. Or a store would sell only vegetables, and among them would be French beans, broad beans, cluster beans, cauliflower, cucumber, bell peppers, *brinjal* (eggplant), green chilies (mild and hot), three different kinds of gourds, and pumpkins and plantains. My mother would say that with a little imagination you can capture the extraordinary freshness and flavor of the market and release it in your cooking.

In this cookbook I've tried to do just that: to capture the love of cooking I inherited from my mother, of freshness, of family, and, because I have lived with my husband and daughter in America for many years, adapt it for an American kitchen. I've tried to translate the way we cook in India—how we combine tastes such as sweet and sour, hot and cool, using spices and other ingredients—and make it enticing for the home cook who may not be familiar with Indian cooking, or who loves Indian cooking but feels intimidated by the ingredients, or who wants to use

Western ingredients and cook them in an Indian fashion. I've tried to include the new with the traditional, the Western with the Eastern. And Indian cooking is nutritionally sound, full of complex carbohydrates such as grains and legumes, and including fruits, vegetables, yogurt, and milk. It is healthy cooking at its most interesting with full, complex tastes and flavors; there is nothing bland about red hot chilies!

The basics of Indian cooking are simple: Cook with your hands, your eyes, your nose, your ears, and your taste. Often I will describe when something is done by the way it sizzles in the pan or the color it turns or how it feels to the touch. I want you to learn how to use all your five senses to cook, using Indian methods but not strictly Indian ingredients. You may not easily find some of the Indian ingredients in your neighborhood, so when appropriate I've given substitutions such as lime juice for tamarind water or half-and-half for coconut milk. Once you get the hang of it, you'll be able to create your own dishes using your favorite fruits and vegetables and combining the spices in new and innovative ways. As my amma said, the most important ingredient in cooking is love.

HELPFUL HINTS

1.

*Always wash all vegetables and
fruits thoroughly with water, whether
grown organically or not.*

2.

*The preparation and cooking times that
I have provided serve as a guideline—
each cook works at his/her own pace.
Stove tops and ovens tend to vary
in temperature settings.*

3.

*If you are unable to eat hot peppers due to
health reasons or sensitive taste buds, omit
them. I assure you the finished dish will still be
tasty. Remember to decrease the amount of salt
if you decide to use fewer hot peppers.*

Indian Vegetarian Cooking from an American Kitchen

CHAPTER I

THE STAPLES OF AN INDIAN KITCHEN

····

SPICES AND SEASONINGS

YOGURT, GHEE, CHEESES, AND MILK SAUCE

RELISHES

CHUTNEYS

PICKLES

MASALA POWDERS

TAMARIND WATER

SPROUTING PULSES

SAUCES

THE STAPLES OF
AN INDIAN KITCHEN

ASAFETIDA · (Heeng)

Asafetida is a brown resin obtained from the roots of a certain Indian plant. It is available either in lump form (its purest state) or powdered, which is more convenient to use. Asafetida releases its characteristic smell only when powdered.

Asafetida's distinctive, pungent flavor and aroma is used to season dal or lentil dishes, chutneys, and so on. It has strong digestive properties and is used to counteract flatulence.

Asafetida is prepared by adding only ⅛ teaspoon to 1 teaspoon hot vegetable oil. Heat until it releases its strong odor, usually after only a few seconds.

BAY LEAF · (Tej Patta)

There are two kinds of bay leaves. The Indian bay leaf comes from the cassia tree and has a sweet taste with a spicy aroma. It is mainly used in the preparation of meat dishes. The other variety comes from the bay tree, native to China and southeast Asia, and has a bitter taste with a lemony aroma. Use the latter variety in smaller quantities.

CARDAMOM · (Elaichi)

The fruit of the cardamom plant, the cardamom pod, comes in two colors: green and black. The black cardamom is available in Indian and specialty stores. It is sold only in the whole form, although it is used either whole or powdered to prepare garam masala, relishes, and rice pilafs. Black cardamom has a nuttier flavor than green cardamom, which can be substituted if the black is unavailable.

Green cardamom has a pale green skin and a sweet taste and is available either whole or powdered. It is mainly used in flavoring puddings, sweets, and many classic vegetarian dishes.

Cardamoms can be added along with other spices in preparing tea and are also chewed after dinner as breath fresheners.

CAROM · (Ajwain)

Carom is the seed of the thymol plant, which grows in southern India. The seeds look very much like celery seeds but have a sharp taste and smell like thyme. Carom is used in the preparation of pickles as well as for seasoning many vegetarian dishes.

CILANTRO · (Hara Dhania)

Fresh cilantro leaves, sometimes called fresh coriander, come from the same plant *(Coriandrum sativum)* as coriander seeds. Latino markets and mainstream groceries refer to this plant as "cilantro"; Asian markets will call it "Chinese parsley." Cilantro resembles Italian flat-leaf parsley, although the cilantro leaves are lighter green, thinner, and more fragrant than parsley. Fresh cilantro should be cleaned and stored like fresh parsley.

CINNAMON · (Dalchini)

Cinnamon comes in two varieties. Indian cinnamon is the bark of the cassia tree. The bark is peeled in long strips, called cinnamon sticks. This has a reddish brown color with a sweet, delicate taste and strong aroma. The other cinnamon is the bark of the cinnamon tree. The bark is slender and smooth and has a milder aroma than the Indian variety. They can be used interchangeably.

CLOVE · (Lavang)

Cloves are the dried flower buds of the clove tree. They are dark brown with a sharp taste and available either whole or powdered.

CORIANDER SEED · (Dhania)

Coriander seed is the ripe fruit of the coriander plant. It is round and light brown in color and has a strong, nutty aroma. It is available in three forms: whole, powdered, or ground. It is used to thicken sauces and to season sautéed vegetable dishes. Ground coriander is available in Indian stores and other specialty markets.

CUMIN · (Jeera)

Cumin is the dried ripe fruit of the cumin plant. It comes in two varieties, white and black. In India, it is one of the most widely used spices, whole or powdered. White cumin, commonly referred to as cumin, is actually yellowish brown in color. It resembles the caraway seed in shape, but it is larger in size. Black cumin (known as royal cumin, or shahi jeera) is sweeter than white cumin. This also resembles the caraway seed but is smaller. White cumin is available whole or powdered; black cumin is only available whole.

CURRY LEAVES · (Curry Patta or Meethe Neam ke Patte)

Curry leaves are shiny, thin, and dark green in color; they are used in dal.

FENNEL SEED · (Saunf)

Fennel seed, from the fennel plant, has a sweet licorice or anise taste. It is used whole or powdered. The thinner seed, known as lakhnawi saunf, is served as an after-dinner mint.

FENUGREEK · (Methi)

Fenugreek seed *(Trigonella foenumgraecum)* is a small legume with a bitter taste. It is used both whole and powdered, and is usually dry-roasted to enhance its flavor. Fresh fenugreek leaves are slightly bitter and are used to prepare dal stews. Dried leaves are used as herbs.

GINGER· (Adrak)

Fresh ginger is the underground root of the ginger plant *(Aingiber offinale)* grown in Asia. Fresh ginger is used shredded, minced, or pureed. It stays fresh for many days in the refrigerator.

Ginger is also available in a powdered form and is used in sweet pickles and relishes.

MANGO POWDER · (Amchoor)

A tan-colored powder made from peeled, unripe, tart, sun-dried mangoes. It has a pungent aroma and a sour taste and is used instead of lime juice or tamarind. It is available in Indian grocery stores.

MUSTARD · (Rai)

The seed from the mustard plant, *Brassica juncea,* is tiny, round, and brownish-black or purplish-black. Black mustard seeds, ground or cooked, impart a spicy flavor. It can be used, whole or powdered, to prepare pickles as well as other vegetable dishes.

NUTMEG · (Jaiphul)

Nutmeg is the dark brown nut enclosed within the mace membrane. The shell is dried, then grated into a powder. Nutmeg is available either whole or powdered. Its sweet taste and mild fragrance is used in the preparation of relishes and garam masala.

PAPRIKA· (Deghi Mirch)

The chili pod of the plant capsicum is sun-dried and ground to produce mild red chili powder, similar to Hungarian paprika. It turns food a brilliant red.

POMEGRANATE · (Anardana)

These plump seeds are enclosed in the honeycombed membrane of the deep red fruit. The seeds can be eaten raw, or dried and used as a spice. Dried, powdered pomegranate is used in Indian cooking.

POPPY SEED, WHITE · (Khas-Khas)

The white seeds from the poppy plant are available whole, and when raw their taste is very mild; when roasted, the seeds are ground with other spices to season primarily vegetable dishes.

RED PEPPER · (Lal Mirch)

Red pepper, the ripe, sun-dried chili pod of the capsicum plant, is available whole, as a pod, or in flakes. The spicy red pepper is an essential ingredient in Indian cooking.

SAFFRON · (Kesar)

Saffron is the dried stigma of the flower of the saffron plant *(Crocus sativus)*. It is one of the most expensive spices in the world and is available either in reddish-brown threads or powdered. It imparts a beautiful orange-yellow color to a dish. Because of its strong flavor, it should be used sparingly. Saffron is used in puddings, sweets, and pilafs.

TAMARIND · (Imli)

Tamarind is the pulpy pod of the tropical plant *Tamarindus indica,* grown in India. It is brownish-black in color and tastes tart. The ripe tamarind pods are peeled and pitted, and the pulp compressed into small cakes. Tamarind is widely used in southern India to prepare lentils, chutneys, and vegetable dishes. It is also available in the form of paste at Asian grocery stores (tamarind paste).

TURMERIC · (Haldi)

Turmeric is the root of the tropical plant *Curcuma longa.* The roots are cleaned, boiled, dried, and pulverized into an aromatic yellow powder. It is mainly used in dals and vegetable dishes to impart a characteristic yellow color.

YOGURT, GHEE, CHEESES, AND MILK SAUCE

YOGURT (DAHI)

*Y*ogurt is used in Indian cooking to prepare cold drinks (lassi), dressing for salads (raita), relishes, sauces, and soups.

While yogurt is readily available in supermarkets, homemade yogurt is definitely tastier, fresher, and more economical than commercial brands. There are yogurt makers available for home use, but to make yogurt you really don't need one. Any bowl—glass, china, Pyrex, stainless steel—with a lid can be used. Yogurt sets best when the temperature of the milk is around 105 degrees; at this temperature the yogurt culture is added. Place the bowl of milk in a gas oven with the pilot light on, or on a low-set heating pad, or near a radiator—as long as the temperature of 75–80 degrees is maintained; too cold, the yogurt will not set, too hot, the yogurt will turn sour.

> *1 quart (4 cups) milk (whole, 2%,*
> * 1%, or skim, according to your*
> * preference)*
> *2 Tbsp. plain yogurt*

In a heavy-bottomed saucepan, bring the milk to a boil. Once the milk begins to rise in the pan, turn off the heat and let it cool to 105 degrees. Pour the milk in a bowl. Add the yogurt, cover, and leave in a warm place where the temperature is maintained around 75–80 degrees. Leave it to set undisturbed for about 7 or 8 hours. Homemade yogurt will keep in the refrigerator for 3 days.

YOGURT CHEESE

*Y*ogurt cheese tastes better and has fewer calories than commercial cream cheese. It is very easy to make. Whole milk yogurt makes a creamier cheese, but it can be made with low-fat and nonfat yogurt as well. This soft cheese is excellent for dips, salads, and spreads.

MAKES 1 CUP

> *2 cups (16 oz.) plain yogurt*

Line a strainer with either a double layer of cheesecloth or a paper coffee filter. Set the strainer in a bowl deep enough for the yogurt to drip into. Put the yogurt in the strainer and let it drain into the bowl overnight in the refrigerator. Spoon the cheese from the filter or cheesecloth into a container. You can either refrigerate it, covered, as is or season the cheese to taste with salt, white pepper, herbs, or chopped scallions or cilantro, then cover and refrigerate.

CLARIFIED BUTTER (GHEE)

1 pound (4 sticks) unsalted butter

In a heavy-bottomed saucepan, heat the butter over medium-low heat. Once the butter melts a thin layer of white foam forms on the top. After 10 minutes, the foam subsides. As soon as the butter fat residue starts to brown, the foam forms on the top again. Push the foam aside to see if the bottom residue is brown. If so, turn off the heat. Let cool. The butter has now separated into clear liquid on top and brown residue on the bottom. Pour the clear liquid into a jar through a fine sieve or through a double layer of cheesecloth. Make sure that the brown residue from the bottom is kept separate and is discarded. Let the clear liquid cool completely. Cover. Ghee keeps for 4 to 6 weeks on the counter or 2 to 3 months in the refrigerator.

INDIAN CHEESE (CHENNA AND PANEER)

Chenna is a fine-grained homemade Indian cheese, very similar to pot cheese or ricotta cheese, but much drier. Chenna is used primarily in sweets.

When chenna is compressed into a cake and cut into small rectangles it is called paneer. Paneer acts like a sponge, soaking up the flavor of whatever spices it is cooked with. It is used in savory dishes such as Green Peas and Homemade Cheese in Tomato Sauce (Matar Paneer, page 118) or Spinach with Homemade Cheese (Saag Paneer, page 119).

2 quarts (8 cups) whole milk
¼ cup lemon juice or 1 cup plain
   lowfat yogurt

1. In a heavy-bottomed saucepan, bring the milk to a boil. Reduce the heat and slowly add the lemon juice or yogurt, stirring gently with a spoon. As soon as white curds form, separating from the yellow whey, turn off the heat. Cover and leave it on the counter to set for 10 minutes.

2. If after 10 minutes you see only a few curds of chenna and most of the liquid is still milky, repeat the process, adding a little more lemon juice or yogurt.

3. Line a colander or sieve with a triple layer of cheesecloth, and put it in the sink. Pour the curds and the whey into the sieve, draining the whey. A convenient way to drain the cheese further is to gather up the four corners of the cheesecloth and tie them together with a piece of string long enough to secure to the faucet. Let it hang on the faucet for 2 hours to drain. Then squeeze out as much liquid as possible.

4. This moist, drained cheese is chenna. Turn chenna out onto a clean, dry work surface and knead for 10 to 15 minutes, until the texture is fine and slightly grainy.

5. To make paneer, hang the chenna bundle on the kitchen faucet or over a bowl overnight. In the morning, untie the bundle. Leaving the cheese in the cheesecloth, flatten it by placing a heavy object, such as soup cans or a pot filled with water, on top of the cheese for 2 hours. This compressed cheese should be about ½ to ¾ inch thick.

6. Remove the cheese from the cheesecloth and cut into cubes with a sharp knife. Paneer keeps for 4 days in the refrigerator. It is very delicate and is usually fried with a little oil, butter, or ghee to a golden brown and then used to finish a dish. Paneer, like tofu, is full of protein but essentially tasteless. The taste comes from the flavors of the food with which it is cooked.

THICKENED MILK SAUCE (RABADI)

*R*abadi is traditionally used in desserts such as a pudding with nuts (Cream Pudding, page 225).

MAKES 2 CUPS

2 quarts (8 cups) milk

In a heavy-bottomed saucepan, bring the milk to a boil. Lower the heat and simmer, stirring constantly to ensure that the milk doesn't stick to the bottom of the pan. After 45 minutes the milk should be reduced to 2¼ cups and have the consistency of a thick cream sauce. Cool, then refrigerate.

RELISHES

In Indian cooking, vegetable relishes are used as condiments or accompaniments to main dishes. The vegetables are chopped or grated and seasoned with a dash of salt, pepper, or lime juice. The following recipes make 2 cups.

A NOTE ABOUT HOT PEPPERS: Many of the recipes call for hot peppers, such as jalapeños or green chilies. Please exercise caution when cooking with hot peppers. Be sure to wash your hands thoroughly after handling them, being careful not to touch your face or especially your eyes after touching the seeds. You may want to use rubber gloves when handling the peppers to prevent an accident. If you have never eaten a dish with hot peppers, it is best to use hot peppers sparingly until your palate gets accustomed to them. In the recipes in this book, I have given the option of how many peppers to include according to your taste.

RAW ONION RELISH

2 red or Vidalia onions, peeled and
    thinly sliced
1 green chili pepper, seeded and
    sliced

1 Tbsp. lime or lemon juice
Salt to taste

Rinse the onion slices in cold water three or four times. Gently squeeze out excess water and put in a bowl. Stir in the chili pepper, lime juice, and salt. Refrigerate.

ONION, TOMATO, AND CUCUMBER RELISH

*1 tomato, seeded, pulped, and
sliced*
*1 red onion, peeled and thinly
sliced*
*1 pickle or kirby cucumber, peeled,
seeded, and cut into ¼ inch dice*
*1 green bell pepper, seeded and
finely chopped*

⅛ tsp. cayenne pepper
¼ tsp. ground cumin
1 Tbsp. lime or lemon juice
1 Tbsp. chopped fresh cilantro
Salt to taste

In a bowl, combine all the ingredients. Stir. Refrigerate for 15 minutes or until ready to serve.

GRATED CUCUMBER RELISH

*6 kirby cucumbers (any other
variety, 2 cucumbers)*
*1 jalapeño pepper, seeded and
minced*

1 Tbsp. lime or lemon juice
1 Tbsp. chopped fresh cilantro
⅛ tsp. freshly ground black pepper
Salt to taste

Peel, half, and seed the cucumbers. Grate the cucumbers into a bowl. Cover and refrigerate. When you are ready to serve, squeeze excess moisture from cucumbers and stir in the lime or lemon juice, cilantro, pepper, and salt.

SHREDDED CARROT AND ONION RELISH

4 carrots, peeled and finely grated
*1 red onion, peeled and finely
chopped*
1 Tbsp. lime or lemon juice

2 green chilies, seeded and chopped
1 Tbsp. chopped fresh cilantro
Salt to taste

In a bowl, mix all the ingredients except the salt. Cover and refrigerate. When you are ready to serve, add salt and stir. If you do not like the taste of raw carrots, you can stir-fry the grated carrots with 1 teaspoon of vegetable oil for 5 minutes. Proceed with the recipe.

CHUTNEYS

Chutneys are wonderful accompaniments to breads, dal, rice, and vegetable dishes. Like relishes, chutneys rely on hot peppers for some of their flavor.

FRESH COCONUT AND MINT CHUTNEY

*W*hile fresh coconut is preferable, frozen grated coconut is available in Hispanic grocery stores and some supermarkets. If neither fresh nor frozen coconut is available, you can use dried, powdered, or flaked unsweetened coconut instead.

MAKES 1½ CUPS

1 cup fresh or defrosted frozen coconut
8 fresh mint leaves
¼ cup fresh cilantro
1–2 jalapeño peppers, with or without seeds according to taste
2 tsp. brown sugar

½ inch fresh ginger, peeled
1 Tbsp. fresh lime juice or ½ tsp. tamarind paste
8 unsalted cashews
Salt to taste
¼ cup water

In a blender or food processor fitted with a steel blade, process all ingredients to a smooth, creamy puree. Serve either chilled or at room temperature. To use as a dipping sauce for fried appetizers, add a little more water to thin the puree.

FRESH COCONUT, FRESH CILANTRO, AND TAMARIND CHUTNEY

This chutney is a must for masala dosas (page 204), and it also goes well with samosas or any savory fritters; or serve it as a dipping sauce for raw vegetables. Chana is a legume available in Indian grocery stores. If chana is unavailable you can substitute yellow split peas.

2 Tbsp. chana dal or yellow split peas	½ tsp. salt
1 cup grated fresh coconut	1 tsp. tamarind paste
2 green chilies or jalapeño peppers, stemmed	1 tsp. brown sugar
½ cup chopped fresh cilantro	8 unsalted cashews
	½ cup water

In a small saucepan over medium heat, roast chana dal until it turns a shade darker, about 1 minute. In a blender or food processor fitted with a steel blade, process dal, coconut, pepper, cilantro, salt, tamarind paste, brown sugar, cashews, and water to a creamy, smooth puree. Store in a container.

The traditional way of finishing this dish is by adding the following seasoning:

2 tsp. vegetable oil
1 tsp. black mustard seeds
10 fresh curry leaves, if available
¼ tsp. ground asafetida

In a small saucepan with a lid, heat the oil. Once the oil is hot, add the mustard seeds and cover until you hear the seeds sputter. Reduce the heat; add the curry leaves and asafetida. Turn off the heat and pour this on the chutney and stir. Cover and refrigerate. This chutney keeps for 2 days.

FRESH MINT CHUTNEY (PUDINA CHUTNEY)

Fresh mint chutney is one of the most popular chutneys. Its clean, sharp taste makes it an excellent accompaniment to any dish: rice, bread, or fried savories. This chutney *must* be made with fresh mint.

MAKES 1½ CUPS

2 cups fresh mint leaves
½–1 tsp. crushed red pepper, to taste
2 Tbsp. lime juice
½ cup dried coconut

¼ cup water
1 tsp. salt
1 tsp. brown sugar
2 tsp. vegetable oil or olive oil

In a blender or food processor fitted with a steel blade, puree all of the ingredients, except the oil. Heat the oil in a small saucepan. Add the chutney carefully, making sure the hot oil does not spatter, and stir-fry for 10 minutes until the mixture turns pale green and releases a minty aroma. Let it cool. Transfer to a bowl and refrigerate, covered. This chutney stays fresh in the refrigerator for 1 week.

FRESH CILANTRO CHUTNEY

This chutney goes well with any vegetable fritters and is excellent as a dipping sauce.

MAKES 1 CUP

½ cup grated fresh coconut
¼ cup unsalted chopped cashews
1 cup loosely packed fresh cilantro
1–3 green chilies or jalapeño
    peppers, tops removed,
    according to taste
½ inch fresh ginger, peeled and
    chopped

¼ cup water
1 tsp. brown sugar
1 tsp. salt
2 Tbsp. fresh lime juice or 1 tsp.
    tamarind paste

In a blender or food processor fitted with a steel blade, puree all the ingredients. Pour into a bowl, cover, and refrigerate. This keeps for 2 days. Remove from the refrigerator half an hour before serving.

SOUR MANGO CHUTNEY

*T*here are two varieties of mangoes. One is green and firm and considered "raw mango"; it is used for chutney and pickles. The fresh, sweet mangoes are red and eaten as fruit. This recipe calls for the raw mango.

MAKES 2 CUPS

*2 firm, raw mangoes (about
   2 lbs.)
½ tsp. cayenne pepper, or more to
   taste
½ tsp. salt*

*2 Tbsp. brown sugar
1 tsp. ground cumin
1 tsp. ground coriander
½ tsp. powdered ginger*

Peel and seed the mangoes; cut the pulp into ½-inch pieces. In a blender or food processor fitted with a steel blade, puree the mangoes, cayenne pepper, salt, brown sugar, cumin, coriander, and ginger. Taste for tartness. If too sour, add more brown sugar and process another minute. For extra spiciness, add dried red pepper. Cover and refrigerate. Although this chutney tastes best when freshly prepared, it will keep in the refrigerator for 4 days.

HOT TOMATO CHUTNEY

*M*ake this chutney when tomatoes are in season and serve it with bread, dal, or vegetable dishes.

MAKES 1 CUP

1 Tbsp. vegetable oil or olive oil
1 tsp. cumin seeds
1–2 jalapeño peppers or green
    chilies, sliced, to taste
2 whole dried red chilies
1 lb. ripe tomatoes, cored and
    coarsely chopped

3 Tbsp. brown sugar
¼ tsp. ground cinnamon
¼ tsp. black pepper
½ tsp. salt

In a large skillet, heat the oil. When the oil is hot but not smoking, reduce the heat and add the cumin seeds, jalapeño peppers, and dried red chilies, and sauté until the cumin seeds darken and turn brown. Reduce the heat to medium-low and add the tomatoes, brown sugar, cinnamon, pepper, and salt, and cook, stirring, for 15 minutes until chutney thickens. Serve warm or chilled. This chutney will keep in the refrigerator for 3 days.

SWEET TOMATO CHUTNEY

*T*his chutney goes well on toasted bread. If you want to make it spicier, add more red peppers and ¼ teaspoon garam masala. It takes about 40 minutes to prepare.

MAKES 1 CUP

1 lb. ripe tomatoes, peeled, cored,
    seeded, and chopped
1 red onion, peeled and finely
    chopped
2 cloves garlic, peeled and minced
½ cup white wine vinegar or cider
    vinegar

¼ tsp. cayenne pepper or paprika
½ tsp. powdered ginger
½ cup brown sugar
¼ tsp. freshly ground black pepper
¼ tsp. ground cumin
½ tsp. salt

In a large, heavy-bottomed, nonreactive pot, bring all the ingredients to a boil. Reduce heat to medium-low and simmer for 30 minutes, until the sauce becomes fairly thick and glossy and is no longer watery. Taste for salt and sugar as needed. Let cool completely and refrigerate. In a tightly sealed, sterilized jar, refrigerated, this chutney stays fresh for a month.

FRESH PINEAPPLE AND RAISIN CHUTNEY

This spicy chutney is an excellent accompaniment for any vegetable dish.

MAKES 2 CUPS

1 ripe pineapple, peeled, cored, diced, with its juice
½ cup golden raisins
2 jalapeño peppers, stems removed, seeded if desired, and minced
1–2 dried red peppers or ½ tsp. crushed red pepper
1 red onion, peeled and finely chopped
1 red bell pepper, seeded and finely chopped
2 cloves garlic, peeled and minced
1 tsp. ground cumin
1 tsp. ground coriander
¼ tsp. ground cloves
2 Tbsp. brown sugar
½ cup white wine vinegar
Salt to taste

In a heavy-bottomed nonreactive pot, bring all the ingredients to a boil. Reduce the heat and simmer for 45 minutes until the chutney is thick and glossy. Cool to room temperature. This chutney keeps, refrigerated, for 2 weeks.

SWEET AND SOUR TAMARIND CHUTNEY (IMLI CHUTNEY)

This chutney is the best accompaniment to savory samosas, pastries with spicy potato and pea filling (page 44). Tamarind is available in specialty Asian markets.

MAKES 2 CUPS

1 small lime-size tamarind pulp
¼ cup brown sugar
¾ cup chopped pitted dates

1 tsp. dry-roasted cumin seeds
¼ tsp. cayenne pepper (optional)
1 tsp. salt

Soak the tamarind in a bowl with 1 cup of boiling water for 15 minutes. Mash the pulp with the back of a spoon or with your fingers to a thick, lumpy consistency. In a blender or food processor fitted with a steel blade, puree the pulp, brown sugar, dates, cumin seeds, cayenne, and salt. Covered and refrigerated, this chutney stays fresh for 2 weeks.

FRESH GINGER AND COCONUT CHUTNEY

This is a spicy chutney that can be served with any mild dish and is a terrific dipping sauce for vegetable fritters.

MAKES 1 CUP

1 cup dried coconut powder or
½ cup unsalted cashews
2 inches fresh ginger, peeled and
sliced
1 tsp. tamarind paste or 1 Tbsp.
lime juice

6 dried red hot peppers or
3 jalapeño peppers, stemmed
1 tsp. salt
⅓ cup water
2 tsp. vegetable oil

1. In a blender or food processor fitted with a steel blade, puree all the ingredients, except the oil.
2. In a saucepan, heat the oil and carefully add the puree. Sauté for 5 minutes, until the mixture releases the smell of ginger. Remove from the heat and let cool. Serve at room temperature. This keeps fresh refrigerated for 1 week.

PICKLES (ACHAR)

Achar, or pickles, are fruit or vegetables steeped in salt, vinegar, and spices; they are used as a flavorful accompaniment to any meal. While many varieties of pickles are available in Indian grocery stores, they are easy to make at home. Although they are time-consuming to prepare, nothing beats the superb flavor of homemade pickles.

HOT LEMON PICKLE (NIMBOO KA ACHAR)

Although this is called Hot Lemon Pickle, I prefer the taste of limes to lemons. This pickle goes well with yogurt rice or toast.

MAKES 2 CUPS

4 fresh limes
3 Tbsp. salt

1 tsp. ground turmeric
½ tsp. ground asafetida

SPICE MIXTURE:
½ tsp. black mustard seeds
1 tsp. fenugreek seeds

TO PREPARE THE PICKLE:
½ cup vegetable oil or peanut oil
1 tsp. cayenne pepper

1. Wash the limes and wipe them completely dry because any moisture will spoil the pickle. Cut the limes in half, then each half into quarters. Put all the lime pieces into a sterilized jar and add the salt; mix and cover the jar with a lid. Keep it in a cool, dry place for a week, stirring the pickles once every 2 days. After a week the lime pieces should be slightly tender.

2. Heat a small sauté pan and add the mustard and fenugreek seeds. Roast over medium heat for 5 minutes, until the mustard seeds turn gray and the fenugreek seeds turn dark brown. Add the turmeric and asafetida, and roast for 10 seconds. Take off the heat and let cool. In a coffee grinder or with a mortar and pestle, grind the spices to a fine powder. Set aside.

3. To prepare the pickle:

Heat the oil in a small saucepan and turn off the heat. Add the spice mixture to the hot oil, stir, and pour over the lime pieces along with the cayenne pepper. Mix well. This pickle keeps for months in the refrigerator.

RAW MANGO PICKLE (AAM KA ACHAR)

Fresh raw mangoes are available only in spring and summer—the best time to prepare this pickle. Unlike the previous recipe, this pickle does not require a week-long steep. You can serve it immediately with any vegetable dish and yogurt rice.

MAKES 3 CUPS

2 raw mangoes
1 to 2 Tbsp. salt
1 tsp. cayenne pepper

FOR THE SEASONING:
2 Tbsp. light vegetable oil
1 tsp. black mustard seeds
½ tsp. ground asafetida
8–10 fresh curry leaves (optional)

1. Wash the mangoes and wipe them completely dry. Even the slightest bit of moisture can spoil the pickle. Do not peel the mangoes. Cut the mangoes into ½-inch cubes and discard the seed. Put the cubes in a glass bowl and add the salt and cayenne pepper. Mix well.
2. In a small pan, heat the oil. When hot add the mustard seeds. Because the seeds will pop and sputter, cover the pan with a lid. When the seeds stop sputtering, add the asafetida (and the curry leaves if desired). Once the mixture starts to sizzle, turn off the heat. Pour the contents of the pan over the mango pieces and mix well. This pickle keeps for 2 to 3 weeks in the refrigerator.

JALAPEÑO PEPPERS IN VINEGAR

Raw, these peppers are very hot, but they lose their bite when they are marinated in white wine vinegar. You can use these hot peppers in a salad or sandwich or to perk up any mild vegetable dish. See note on handling hot peppers, page 13.

MAKES 2 CUPS

1 lb. jalapeño peppers
1 bottle (16 oz.) distilled white
wine vinegar

2 Tbsp. salt
½ tsp. freshly ground black pepper
½ tsp. ground asafetida

1. Wash the jalapeño peppers and drain in a colander for an hour. Pour the vinegar, salt, black pepper, and asafetida into a sterilized jar.
2. Dry the peppers thoroughly with paper towels. Holding the stem, cut each pepper into ¼-inch rounds. Discard the stems. Put the slices in the jar with the vinegar mixture. Cover the jar with a lid and shake vigorously to mix. Set aside for 4 to 5 days until the peppers turn pale, losing their bright green color.
3. This pickle will keep fresh in the refrigerator for months.

MASALA POWDERS

The word *masala* means "spices." These powders are prepared by roasting spices and then grinding them to a fine texture. Masala powders are available in Indian grocery stores and many specialty stores. But with a sauté pan and a coffee grinder, it is easy to make your own masala powders. The general procedure is to dry-roast them by stirring the spices in a sauté pan over medium heat for about 4 to 5 minutes. When the spices turn a shade darker and emit a distinct aroma, turn off the heat and let them cool. Grind them to a fine powder. In an airtight jar, the flavor stays fresh for about 4 months.

ROASTED CUMIN POWDER (BHOONA JIRA)

MAKES ½ CUP

Dry-roast and grind ½ cup of cumin seeds according to the general procedure, as described above.

ROASTED CORIANDER AND CUMIN POWDER (DHANIA-JIRA POWDER)

MAKES 1 CUP

This simple combination of spices is used in many sautéed vegetable dishes. Dry-roast and grind ¾ cup coriander seeds and ¼ cup cumin seeds according to the general procedure, as described on page 24.

BASIC CURRY POWDER

MAKES ½ CUP

3 Tbsp. coriander seeds
1 Tbsp. cumin seeds
¼ tsp. black peppercorns

¼ tsp. fenugreek seeds
¼ tsp. mustard seeds
6–8 dried red chilies

Dry-roast and grind all the ingredients according to the general procedure, as described on page 24. In an airtight container, stored in a cool, dry place, curry powder keeps for 6 months.

GARAM MASALA

Garam masala means "hot spices"—a common term used for a combination of many ground spices. I call this "Grand Masala" because a pinch of this makes any mild dish grand.

MAKES ½ CUP

1 Tbsp. vegetable oil	*2 Tbsp. green cardamom seeds*
3 cinnamon sticks, 3 inches long,	*1 Tbsp. whole black peppercorns*
chopped	*1 Tbsp. whole cloves*

In a saucepan, heat the oil. Add the cinnamon sticks and sauté until they release their aroma. With a slotted spoon, remove the cinnamon sticks, and repeat the procedure with the cardamom seeds and the peppercorns. When sautéeing the cloves, use a lid to cover the pan, as they have a tendency to spatter. Combine the roasted spices and grind them to a powder in a coffee grinder. Garam masala keeps for 2 months in an airtight container.

NOTE: You can use store-bought ground cinnamon, cardamom, peppercorns, and cloves, but the result definitely will not have the same pungency or taste as home-ground garam masala.

TAMARIND WATER

MAKES ½ CUP

1 small lime-size tamarind pulp or
1 Tbsp. tamarind paste

Soak the tamarind pulp or paste in boiling water for 15 minutes to soften. Squeeze the tamarind, getting as much juice as possible. Strain through a sieve, discarding the residue. Covered, tamarind water keeps in the refrigerator for 4 days.

SPROUTING PULSES

A pulse is the edible seed of such pod plants as peas, beans, or lentils. The whole mung bean, chickpeas, dried peas, and black-eyed peas are the best pulses to sprout, and they taste delicious in salads or in a side dish with vegetables. Most people are familiar with the store-bought "bean sprouts" made with mung beans. They are easy to make at home.

½ cup mung beans

Here are two methods for making them sprout:

1. Soak the beans in lukewarm water to cover for 6 hours, or preferably overnight. Drain and tie the beans loosely in a cheesecloth and leave them in a warm place. Moisten the cheesecloth with water now and then until the beans sprout.

2. Or, soak the beans as directed above. Drain them and put them in a small bowl. Cover with an inverted bigger bowl and leave in a warm place. Sprinkle water over the beans three or four times—about every 6 hours—until they begin to sprout. Depending on the type of pulse and the room temperature, it usually takes about 36 to 48 hours. The sprouts stay fresh in the refrigerator for about 4 days.

SAUCES

SPICY TOMATO SAUCE

MAKES 2 CUPS

1 Tbsp. vegetable oil
1 onion, peeled and finely chopped
2 cloves garlic, peeled and minced
4 ripe tomatoes, chopped

¼ to ½ tsp. chili powder
1 tsp. brown sugar
½ tsp. salt

1. In a saucepan, heat the oil and add the onion and garlic. Sauté for 3 minutes. Add the tomatoes and simmer until soft. In an electric blender, food processor, or food mill, puree the mixture. (Your choice of equipment depends on your preference—smooth or chunky sauce.)

2. Return the mixture to the stove and add the chili powder, brown sugar, and salt, and bring to a boil. Turn the heat to medium-low and simmer for 10 minutes. Refrigerated, this sauce keeps for a week. Frozen, it keeps for a month.

WHITE SAUCE

*T*here are many recipes for white sauces, most of them highly caloric. This is a low-calorie white sauce, using rice flour or all-purpose flour as a thickening agent.

MAKES 1 CUP

1 Tbsp. rice flour or all-purpose
flour
1½ cups low-fat milk or evaporated
skim milk

Pinch of salt and white pepper

In a small saucepan over low heat, dry-roast the rice flour for 1 minute, taking care not to brown the flour. Slowly add the milk to the pan, stirring constantly to prevent lumps until the sauce is smooth and thickened. Add the salt and pepper, and heat for 1 minute.

CHAPTER 2

APPETIZERS

....

BATTER-COATED SPICY MASHED POTATO BALLS
BREAD FRITTERS
CHILI-CHEESE FRITTERS

APPETIZERS

*T*hese delicately flavored appetizers, easy to prepare, are a terrific prelude to any meal. You can capture the variety and versatility of vegetables in preparing these palate-pleasers. Feel free to serve them as a great snack or as a side dish too!

••••

SPICY CORN ON THE COB

*C*orn on the cob might seem to taste best grilled, but you can get equally delicious results from baking this recipe in the oven. I've given you two kinds of basting sauces: one spicy, one mild and sweet.

PREPARATION TIME: *10 minutes* COOKING TIME: *50 minutes* SERVES: 4

> 4 ears of fresh corn, husks and silk
>   removed
> Green Chili Basting Sauce or Sweet
>   Basting Sauce (recipes follow)

1. Preheat the oven to 400 degrees.
2. With a pastry brush, apply your preferred sauce evenly over each ear of corn. Wrap each cob loosely in heavy aluminum foil, so that there is enough room for heat to circulate. Cook for 45 to 50 minutes until corn is tender.

Green Chili Basting Sauce

2 tsp. olive oil
1–4 green chilies or jalapeño
  peppers, stemmed, to taste
¼ tsp. chili powder
¼ tsp. freshly ground black pepper
¼ tsp. ground cumin

1 tsp. honey
⅛ tsp. salt
1 Tbsp. fresh lime juice
1 Tbsp. finely chopped fresh
  cilantro

In a food processor, puree all the ingredients to a coarse consistency.

Sweet Basting Sauce

2 tsp. olive oil
2 tsp. honey
¼ tsp. ground cinnamon
¼ tsp. freshly ground black pepper

1 Tbsp. finely chopped fresh
  cilantro
⅛ tsp. salt

Mix all the ingredients.

Per ear of corn:
  128 calories, 3g protein, 20g carbohydrate, 4g fat, 13mg sodium, 0mg
  cholesterol, 2g fiber

VEGETABLE KABOBS

*V*ariety and a creamy, exotic baste perk up these vegetable kabobs. For best results, choose fresh, seasonal vegetables for this dish.

PREPARATION TIME: *15 minutes* COOKING TIME: *10 to 12 minutes* SERVES: *4*

FOR THE BASTE:
2 Tbsp. honey
2 Tbsp. Dijon-style mustard
1 clove garlic, peeled and minced
2 Tbsp. virgin olive oil
¼ tsp. cayenne pepper
Salt to taste

FOR THE KABOBS:
16 broccoli florets

1 red onion, peeled and cut into
   wedges
1 red bell pepper, seeded and cut
   into 1-inch squares
1 green bell pepper, seeded and cut
   into 1-inch squares
2 carrots, peeled and cut into
   2-inch pieces
2 zucchini, cut into 1-inch pieces

1. Mix all the baste ingredients in a jar with a tight-fitting lid. Shake well. Refrigerate for an hour to blend the flavors.
2. Prepare an outdoor grill or a stove-top grill.
3. Thread broccoli, onion, bell peppers, carrots, and zucchini alternating on skewers. Brush the vegetables with the baste and grill on a medium-hot grill for 10 to 12 minutes, until the vegetables are tender. If not serving immediately, wrap the cooked kabobs in aluminum foil to keep them warm.

PER SERVING:
119 calories, 4g protein, 19g carbohydrates, 3g fat, 28mg sodium, 0mg cholesterol, 2g fiber

MUSHROOM AND TOMATO TOAST

Tender mushrooms and ripe tomatoes make this a tempting snack.

PREPARATION TIME: 10 minutes COOKING TIME: 10 minutes SERVES: 4

1 Tbsp. virgin olive oil

1 onion, peeled and finely chopped

1–2 jalapeño peppers, chopped and seeded, to taste (optional)

½ lb. fresh button mushrooms, washed and thinly sliced

1 ripe tomato, chopped

⅛ tsp. chili powder

⅛ tsp. ground coriander

⅛ tsp. ground cumin

Salt to taste

8 slices whole wheat or other firm-textured bread, toasted

1. In a large skillet, heat the oil and add the onion (and the jalapeño peppers, if desired). Sauté for 3 to 4 minutes, until the onion is soft and translucent. Add the mushrooms and tomato and cook, stirring, until mushrooms are soft. Add the chili powder, coriander, cumin, and salt, and sauté for 1 minute more.

2. Spread the mushroom-tomato mixture on 4 slices of toast. Cover with the remaining 4 slices, cut into triangles, and serve.

PER SERVING:

156 calories, 7g protein, 23g carbohydrates, 4g fat, 337mg sodium, 0mg cholesterol, 2.4g fiber

CUCUMBER PIROGUE

𝒯ender kirby cucumbers are best suited for this recipe. If they are not in season, you can use any other variety.

PREPARATION TIME: 10 minutes NO COOKING SERVES: 4

4 kirby cucumbers

4 Tbsp. yogurt cheese (p. 10)

⅛ tsp. chili powder

1 Tbsp. finely chopped fresh dill

1 Tbsp. finely chopped fresh cilantro

Salt to taste

1. Peel the cucumbers, and cut each horizontally in half. Hollow and seed each half. In a small bowl, mix the yogurt cheese, chili powder, dill, cilantro, and salt.

2. Fill the cucumbers with the yogurt cheese mixture and serve.

PER SERVING:
   23 calories, 1.5g protein, 3.5g carbohydrates, 0.3g fat, 122mg sodium,
   1.3mg cholesterol, 1g fiber

STUFFED TOMATOES

*T*his tasty tomato dish makes a great summertime appetizer. You can substitute cherry tomatoes in this recipe.

PREPARATION TIME: *10 minutes* NO COOKING SERVES: 4

8 firm, ripe plum tomatoes or
   16 cherry tomatoes
1 cucumber, peeled, seeded, and
   grated
4 Tbsp. yogurt cheese (p. 10) or
   low-fat cottage cheese

⅛ tsp. chili powder or 2 drops
   cayenne pepper sauce
1 Tbsp. chopped fresh cilantro
Salt to taste

1. Cut each tomato in half lengthwise and scoop out seeds and pulp. Set aside. Squeeze out the excess water from the cucumber and put it in a small bowl. Add the yogurt cheese, chili powder, cilantro, and salt. Mix thoroughly.
2. Fill tomato halves with the mixture and serve.

PER SERVING:
   78 calories, 3g protein, 14g carbohydrates, 1g fat, 144mg sodium, 1.3mg
   cholesterol, 2.9g fiber

CARROT AND YOGURT CHEESE ON TOAST

*T*he sweetness of mildly spiced fresh carrots blends well with the tartness of yogurt cheese.

PREPARATION TIME: *10 minutes* NO COOKING SERVES: 4

2 carrots, peeled and grated
4 Tbsp. yogurt cheese (p. 10)
1 tomato, finely chopped
1 red onion, peeled and finely
    sliced

⅛ tsp. chili powder or paprika
1 Tbsp. chopped fresh cilantro
Salt to taste

8 slices whole wheat bread, toasted

In a small bowl, combine all of the ingredients except toast. Spread the mixture on 4 of the slices of toast and top with the remaining slices. To serve hot, place the sandwiches under a preheated broiler for 1 minute, cut into triangles, and serve.

PER SERVING:
128 calories, 6.5g protein, 24g carbohydrates, 0.8g fat, 365mg sodium, 1.3mg cholesterol, 1.2g fiber

MIXED VEGETABLE SANDWICHES

*M*ildly spiced vegetables make these sandwiches hearty and satisfying.

PREPARATION TIME: *10 minutes* COOKING TIME: *15 minutes* SERVES: 4

1 Tbsp. vegetable oil
1 red onion, peeled and sliced into
thin rounds
1 red or green bell pepper, seeded
and thinly sliced
1 carrot, peeled and finely grated
6 cauliflower florets, cooked
6 broccoli florets, cooked
¼ tsp. chili powder or 4 drops of
cayenne pepper sauce

½ tsp. powdered mustard
½ tsp. brown sugar (optional)
Salt to taste
2 Tbsp. yogurt cheese (p. 10)

8 slices of whole wheat bread,
toasted

1. In a nonstick skillet, heat the oil. Add the onion and bell pepper slices, and sauté for 3 to 4 minutes, until soft. Add the carrot, cooked cauliflower and broccoli florets, chili powder, mustard, brown sugar, and salt. Cook for 2 minutes. Let cool for 5 minutes. Add yogurt cheese and stir.
2. Spread mixture on 4 slices of the toast and top with the remaining slices. Cut into triangles and serve.

PER SERVING:
    134 calories, 7g protein, 25g carbohydrates, 0.8g fat, 360mg sodium, 0.3mg cholesterol, 1.9g fiber

CREAMY CAULIFLOWER ON TOAST

Cauliflower is one of the most versatile vegetables. It tastes great in soups, salads, in main dishes, or just as a snack, as in this recipe. This dish can be prepared on the stove top or in the microwave.

PREPARATION TIME: *15 minutes* COOKING TIME: *20 minutes* SERVES: 4

1 small head cauliflower
1 Tbsp. olive oil
1 onion, peeled and chopped
2 green chilies or jalapeño peppers,
   chopped
1 green bell pepper, seeded and
   chopped

Salt to taste
½ cup evaporated skim milk
2 Tbsp. yogurt cheese (p. 10)
2 Tbsp. grated Parmesan cheese
   (optional)

8 slices whole wheat bread, toasted

Stove-top Method:

1. Chop the cauliflower into small pieces.

2. Fill a large saucepan with enough water to cover the cauliflower. Boil water, then add the cauliflower and simmer for 6 to 8 minutes, until tender. Drain and set aside.

3. In a nonstick sauté pan, heat the oil and add the onion, green chilies, and bell pepper, and stir-fry for 5 to 6 minutes, until the onion is tender. Add the salt, cooked cauliflower, and milk, and heat, stirring, for 5 minutes, until the mixture has a creamy consistency. Remove pan from the heat. Add yogurt cheese (and the Parmesan cheese, if desired) and stir.

4. Spread cauliflower on 4 slices of toast. Top with the remaining 4 slices, serve hot.

OR

Microwave Method:

1. Chop the cauliflower into small pieces.

2. Cook cauliflower in a microwave-safe dish with ¼ cup of water on high (100%) for 6 minutes, until tender. Drain and set aside. In the same dish add the oil, onion, green chilies, and bell pepper. Cook, covered, on high for 4 minutes, until the onion is tender. Add the salt, cooked cauliflower, and milk. Mix well and cook on high (100%) for 3 to 4 minutes. Set aside for 1 minute and add yogurt cheese (and Parmesan, if desired). Stir.

3. Spread cauliflower on 4 slices of toast. Top with the remaining 4 slices and serve hot.

PER SERVING:

191 calories, 10g protein, 29g carbohydrates, 5g fat, 306mg sodium, 3mg cholesterol, 1.7g fiber

CURRIED KIDNEY BEANS

This dish is traditionally served as a bread dip, but for convenience, you can serve it on a roll.

PREPARATION TIME: *10 minutes* COOKING TIME: *15 minutes* SERVES: 4

1 (16 oz.) can red kidney beans
1 Tbsp. olive oil
1 onion, peeled and chopped
2 cloves garlic, peeled and minced
1–2 jalapeño peppers, chopped
½ tsp. chili powder
½ tsp. curry powder
¼ cup spicy tomato sauce (p. 27)

1–2 Tbsp. hot jalapeño relish
   (optional)
Salt to taste
4 rolls, split
2 Tbsp. whipped butter or
   margarine
1 ripe tomato, thinly sliced
1 Tbsp. grated Parmesan cheese

1. In a sieve, drain the beans and rinse them under cold running water. Drain again.
2. In a large nonstick skillet or saucepan, heat the oil. Add the onion, garlic, and jalapeño peppers, and sauté over medium heat for 5 minutes until the onion is limp. Add the beans, chili powder, curry powder, tomato sauce, and salt. (If a hotter sauce is desired, add the jalapeño relish.) Simmer over medium heat for 5 to 7 minutes.
3. While the beans are simmering, scoop out the centers of the rolls to form a hollow. Brush the cut side of the rolls with butter, and toast.
4. Fill the bottom half of each roll with the bean mixture. Garnish with tomato slices and sprinkle with cheese. Broil for 2 minutes until cheese has melted. Replace the roll tops and serve hot.

PER SERVING:
   337 calories, 15g protein, 49g carbohydrates, 9g fat, 350mg sodium, 1mg cholesterol, 8g fiber

CREAMY MUSHROOMS

This versatile dish can be served as an hors d'oeuvre, using toothpicks, as an appetizer, or as a side dish.

PREPARATION TIME: *10 minutes* COOKING TIME: *6 minutes* SERVES: 4

1 lb. fresh button mushrooms
1 Tbsp. virgin olive oil
1 red onion, peeled and chopped
2 Tbsp. yogurt cheese (p. 10)

⅛ tsp. chili powder
⅛ tsp. freshly ground black pepper
Salt to taste
2 Tbsp. chopped fresh cilantro

1. Wipe the mushrooms clean of surface dirt with a damp cloth and set aside.
2. In a nonstick saucepan, heat the oil. Add the onion and sauté for 3 minutes. Add the mushrooms and sauté for 3 minutes, until soft. Add the yogurt cheese, chili powder, pepper, salt, and cilantro; stir well.
3. Serve hot.

PER SERVING:
   62 calories, 2g protein, 4.5g carbohydrates, 4g fat, 111mg sodium, 0.4mg cholesterol, 0.4g fiber

CREAMY CORN ON TOAST

Fresh golden corn makes this dish memorable. It goes well with any bread.

PREPARATION TIME: *10 minutes* COOKING TIME: *10 minutes* SERVES: 4

1 Tbsp. vegetable or olive oil
1 onion, peeled and chopped
1–2 jalapeño peppers, chopped
*1 red or green bell pepper, seeded
    and chopped*
*1 cup fresh corn kernels, lightly
    pureed*

1 ripe tomato, chopped
1 Tbsp. fresh lime juice
Salt to taste

8 slices whole wheat bread, toasted

1. In a nonstick skillet, heat the oil. Add the onion, jalapeño peppers, and bell pepper, and sauté for 4 to 5 minutes until the onion is soft. Add the corn, tomato, lime juice, and salt, and simmer on medium heat for 3 to 5 minutes, until the corn is tender.

2. Spread the corn mixture on each of 4 bread slices. Top with the remaining slices. Serve hot.

PER SERVING:
    198 calories, 6.5g protein, 34g carbohydrates, 4g fat, 375mg sodium, 0mg cholesterol, 1g fiber

CREAMY CORN FILLING FOR TARTLETS

*P*erk up tartlets with this light, tasty filling. You can buy frozen phyllo dough tartlet shells in any large supermarket.

PREPARATION TIME: *10 minutes* COOKING TIME: *10 minutes* SERVES: *5*

FOR THE FILLING:
1 Tbsp. vegetable oil
1 onion, peeled and chopped
1–2 jalapeño peppers, stemmed, seeded, and minced, according to taste
2 cups fresh corn kernels, lightly pureed
1 ripe tomato, chopped
⅛ tsp. freshly ground black pepper

1 Tbsp. fresh lime juice
Salt to taste

4 Tbsp. yogurt cheese (p. 10)
2 Tbsp. chopped fresh cilantro

1 box frozen phyllo dough tartlet shells (15 prebaked shells), thawed at room temperature for 10 minutes (follow directions on box)

1. In a nonstick saucepan, heat the oil. Add the onion and jalapeño peppers, and sauté over medium heat for 3 minutes. Add the corn, tomato, black pepper, lime juice, and salt. Simmer, stirring, for 5 to 7 minutes, until hot. Off the heat, add the yogurt cheese and cilantro. Mix well.
2. Fill the shells with corn mixture and serve hot.

PER SERVING (3 SHELLS):
  98 calories, 2.5g protein, 13.5g carbohydrates, 3.5g fat, 1.3mg cholesterol, 160mg sodium, 2g fiber

MUSHROOMS ON CRACKERS

Turn ordinary crackers into zesty appetizers with this flavorful mushroom topping.

PREPARATION TIME: *10 minutes* COOKING TIME: *10 minutes* SERVES: 4

1 Tbsp. olive oil
1 onion, peeled and chopped
2 cloves garlic, peeled and minced
1–2 jalapeño peppers, chopped
10 oz. fresh mushrooms, cleaned
  and finely chopped
1 Tbsp. unbleached all-purpose
  flour

½ cup evaporated skim milk
¼ tsp. salt
2–4 Tbsp. grated Parmesan cheese
  (optional)

20 water crackers, melba rounds,
  or any party crackers

1. Preheat the oven to 300 degrees.
2. In a nonstick skillet, heat the oil. Add the onion, garlic, and jalapeño peppers, and sauté for 3 minutes. Add the mushrooms and cook until they are tender. Add the flour and brown lightly. Stir in the milk and salt, and simmer for 3 minutes, until the mixture is heated through.
3. Coat a baking sheet with vegetable oil spray. Spoon the mixture on top of the crackers and arrange them on a baking sheet (sprinkle with Parmesan cheese if desired). Bake for 2 to 3 minutes. Serve hot.

PER SERVING (5 CRACKERS WITH FILLING):
  175 calories, 7g protein, 20g carbohydrates, 7g fat, 259mg sodium, 4mg cholesterol, 0.4g fiber

CREAMED CORN ON CRACKERS

Creamy corn mixed with hot and spicy flavors makes a great topping.

PREPARATION TIME: *10 minutes* COOKING TIME: *15 minutes* SERVES: 4

1 Tbsp. virgin olive oil
2 onions, peeled and finely
*   chopped*
2 jalapeño peppers, chopped
1 green or red bell pepper, seeded
*   and chopped*
2 cups fresh corn kernels, lightly
*   pureed with 1 tablespoon whole*
*   milk*
Salt to taste

½ tsp. chili powder
½ tsp. ground cumin
½ tsp. ground coriander
1 Tbsp. fresh lime juice
2 Tbsp. chopped fresh cilantro

20 water crackers, melba rounds,
*   or any fat-free party crackers*
2 Tbsp. Parmesan cheese, grated
*   (optional)*

1. In a nonstick skillet, heat the oil. Add the onions, jalapeño peppers, and bell pepper, and sauté for 3 minutes. Add the corn, salt, chili powder, cumin, coriander, and lime juice. Cook over medium heat until the mixture is hot and the corn is tender. Add the cilantro and stir.

2. Coat a baking sheet with vegetable oil spray. Arrange the crackers on the baking sheet. Spoon the corn mixture on the crackers (sprinkle with Parmesan cheese, if desired) and warm under a preheated broiler or in a preheated 300-degree oven for 2 to 3 minutes. Serve hot.

PER SERVING (5 CRACKERS WITH FILLING):
  245 calories, 6g protein, 37g carbohydrates, 8g fat, 400mg sodium, 2mg cholesterol, 1.9g fiber

SAMOSAS (SAVORY PASTRIES WITH SPICY FILLING)

*S*amosas are triangular, crispy, flaky pastries stuffed with mildly spiced vegetables. While they take some time to prepare, they are definitely worth the effort. You can buy commercially made and frozen samosas at Indian grocery stores.

PREPARATION TIME: *45 minutes*   COOKING TIME: *45 minutes*   SERVES: *4–6*
(MAKES 24 SAMOSAS)

FOR THE PASTRY:

*1½ cups unbleached, all-purpose
   flour*
½ tsp. salt
*4 Tbsp. unsalted butter or
   vegetable shortening*
5–6 Tbsp. warm water

FOR THE STUFFING:

4 all-purpose potatoes
*½ cup shelled fresh or thawed
   frozen peas*
2 Tbsp. vegetable oil
*2 onions, peeled and finely
   chopped*

*1 inch fresh ginger, peeled and
   minced*
*1–2 green chilies or jalapeño
   peppers, finely chopped*
½–1 tsp. ground coriander
½–1 tsp. ground cumin
½–1 tsp. garam masala (p. 25)
¼–½ tsp. cayenne pepper
1½ tsp. salt
*1 Tbsp. fresh lime juice or 2 tsp.
   ground pomegranate seeds*
2 Tbsp. chopped fresh cilantro

1 cup additional flour for dusting
Vegetable oil for deep frying

For the pastry:

1. BY HAND: In a mixing bowl, sift the flour and salt together. Add the butter to the bowl and rub the mixture with your fingers until all the flour in the bowl is evenly coated with butter. It should resemble coarse meal. Add 5 tablespoons water to the mixture, and using your hands, knead the mixture into a soft dough. If the dough feels dry, add the remaining water in droplets until it has the consistency of a soft, pliable dough. (The dough can be prepared a day in advance and refrigerated. Remove the dough from the refrigerator 2 hours before you intend to use it.)

IN A FOOD PROCESSOR: To the bowl fitted with a steel blade, add the flour, salt, and butter. Pulse. When the mixture has the consistency of bread crumbs, slowly add the water through the feed tube. Pulse the machine just until the dough forms a ball on the blade.

On a work surface, knead the dough for 10 minutes until it is firm but very pliable. Wrap the dough in plastic and let it rest for half an hour.

For the stuffing:

2. In a saucepan, put the potatoes and enough water to cover; boil until they are fork-tender. Drain. When they are cool enough to handle, peel them and cut them into ½-inch cubes. Set aside.

3. In another saucepan, put the peas with enough boiling water to cover, and cook until they are tender. Drain.

4. In a nonstick saucepan, heat the vegetable oil. Add the onions, ginger, and green chilies, and sauté until the onions are soft and slightly caramelized. Add the potatoes, peas, coriander, cumin, garam masala, cayenne pepper, salt, and lime juice; mix well. Heat thoroughly. Remove from the heat and let the mixture cool. Add the cilantro and stir. (The stuffing can be made 1 day in advance and refrigerated.)

To prepare the samosas:

5. After the dough has rested, knead for a minute and then divide it into twelve equal portions or balls. Keep them covered.

6. Dust a work surface with flour. Take one ball and roll it out into a 6-inch circle. Cut the circle in half. Each semicircle makes one samosa.

7. Fill a small bowl with water. Using your fingertips, moisten half of the semicircle's straight edge with water. Fold the semicircle into thirds, beginning with the dry half, then the moistened half, so the semicircle forms a cone. Use the moistened edge to seal the cone.

8. Fill the cone with a tablespoon of the stuffing. Moisten the top of the cone with a little water and close it by pinching the edges together. (Make sure the seam is well pressed; otherwise the oil will seep into the pastry during the frying and the samosa may taste greasy.) Prepare the remaining dough in the same manner.

To cook the samosas:

9. In a wok or large frying pan over medium-high heat, heat the oil (about 3 inches deep). When the oil is hot (about 350 degrees), lower four to six samosas, or however many will fit comfortably, into the hot oil and fry them slowly on medium-low heat, turning them often, maintaining the oil temperature at 300 degrees, until they are golden brown on both sides. When they are done, remove them with a slotted spoon and drain on paper towels. Fry the remaining samosas in the same manner.

10. Serve samosas hot or warm with Fresh Mint Chutney (Pudina Chutney, p. 17) or Sweet and Sour Tamarind Chutney (Imli Chutney, p. 20). Samosas can be prepared several hours in advance and refrigerated. Just before serving, reheat them in a preheated 350-degree oven for 6–8 minutes.

PER SAMOSA:
> 90 calories, 1g protein, 8g carbohydrates, 6g fat, 92mg sodium, 5mg cholesterol, 1g fiber

FRITTERS

Fritters are vegetables coated with a spicy chickpea flour (besan) batter and deep-fried. Any vegetables—broccoli, cauliflower, onions, potatoes, spinach, or egg-plant—can be used to make these fritters.

There are two methods of making fritters. Batter-dipped fritters are made by dipping the vegetable in the batter and dropping them in hot oil. Spoon-fried fritters are made by chopping the vegetable and incorporating it into the thick batter. Spoonfuls of batter are then lowered into hot oil and fried over medium-low heat until they are crisp.

Fritters can be prepared well in advance and, just before serving, heat in a pre-heated 350-degree oven for 5 minutes.

CAULIFLOWER FRITTERS (GOBHI PAKORA)

resh cauliflower florets are steamed for a few minutes, then dipped in batter and fried.

PREPARATION TIME: *35 minutes* COOKING TIME: *30 minutes* SERVES: 4 (MAKES 20 FRITTERS)

1 head cauliflower

FOR THE BATTER:
1½ cups chickpea flour (besan)
¼ tsp. cayenne pepper
⅛ tsp. garam masala (p. 25)

1 tsp. salt
2 Tbsp. fresh lime juice
¾ cup water
¼ tsp. baking soda

Vegetable oil for deep-frying

1. Wash the cauliflower, dry it, and cut it into 1-inch florets. Set aside.

2. Into a bowl, sift the chickpea flour. Add the cayenne pepper, garam masala, salt, and lime juice, and stir. Slowly add the water while beating the mixture with a wire whisk, until the batter has the consistency of heavy cream. Cover the bowl and set aside in a warm place for half an hour.

3. When you are ready to fry, add the baking soda to the batter and beat it for 2 minutes.

4. In a wok or a large frying pan, heat the vegetable oil (about 3 inches deep). When the oil is hot but not smoking (360 degrees), dip 4 to 5 pieces of cauliflower in the batter and gently lower the coated florets, one at a time, into the hot oil. (Maintain the oil temperature around 300 degrees—between medium-high and medium-low; it should be gently bubbling.) Fry the fritters for 5 to 7 minutes, until they are golden all over. Remove them with a slotted spoon and drain on paper towels. Continue until all the florets are fried. Serve hot with Fresh Cilantro Chutney and Fresh Mint Chutney (p. 17).

5. Cauliflower fritters can be prepared in advance. Just before serving, heat in a preheated 350-degree oven for 5 minutes.

PER FRITTER:
75 calories, 4g protein, 8g carbohydrates, 3g fat, 61mg sodium, 0mg cholesterol, 2g fiber

ONION FRITTERS (PIAZ PAKORA)

These onion pakoras are just like onion rings: crispy on the outside and delicate on the inside.

PREPARATION TIME: *35 minutes* COOKING TIME: *25 minutes* SERVES: 4 (MAKES 20 FRITTERS)

FOR THE BATTER:
1 cup chickpea flour (besan)
2 Tbsp. rice flour or rice powder
½ tsp. ground cumin
½ tsp. cayenne pepper (or more if
  you like it spicy)

1 Tbsp. fresh lime or lemon juice
½ tsp. salt
¾ cup warm water

2 onions
Vegetable oil for deep-frying

1. Into a bowl, sift the chickpea flour and rice flour. Add the cumin, cayenne pepper, lime juice, and salt. Slowly add the water, beating the batter with a wire whisk, until the batter has the consistency of heavy cream. Whip the batter vigorously for 5 minutes, until it is fluffy, and set aside in a warm place for half an hour.
2. Peel the onions and slice them into very thin rounds. Fold them into the batter.
3. In a wok or a large frying pan, heat the vegetable oil (about 3 inches deep). When the oil is hot but not smoking (360 degrees), gently lower the battered onion rings into the hot oil, four to five fritters at a time. (Maintain the oil temperature at around 300 degrees—between medium-high and medium-low; it should be gently bubbling. This gives the fritters a crunchy coating.) Fry them for 6 to 8 minutes, until they are golden on both sides. Remove them with a slotted spoon and drain on paper towels. Serve hot or warm with either of the coconut chutneys (pp. 15 and 16).

PER FRITTER:
  60 calories, 2.5g protein, 8g carbohydrates, 2g fat, 44mg sodium, 0mg cholesterol, 1.5g fiber

POTATO FRITTERS (ALOO PAKORAS)

Thin-sliced potatoes are batter-fried to a crunchy snack. Any kind of potato can be used for this dish.

PREPARATION TIME: *15 minutes* COOKING TIME: *25 minutes* SERVES: 4 (MAKES 20 FRITTERS)

FOR THE BATTER:
1 cup sifted chickpea flour (besan)
2 Tbsp. rice flour or rice powder
¼–½ tsp. chili powder
1 Tbsp. fresh lime juice
½ tsp. salt

½ cup water
⅛ tsp. baking soda

3 potatoes, peeled and sliced in
  ⅛-inch-thick slices
Vegetable oil for deep-frying

1. Into a bowl, sift the chickpea flour and rice flour. Add the chili powder, lime juice, and salt. Slowly add the water while beating the mixture with a wire whisk, until the batter has the consistency of heavy cream. Cover and set aside for 10 minutes.
2. In a wok or a deep-frying pan, heat the oil (about 3 inches deep). While the oil is heating, add the baking soda to the batter and beat for 1 minute. When the oil is hot but not smoking (around 360 degrees), one at a time, dip the potato slices into the batter and carefully slip them into the hot oil. Fry 6 to 7 potato slices at a time for about 4 to 5 minutes until they are golden on both sides. Maintain the oil temperature at around 300 degrees. As they are done, remove them with a slotted spoon and drain on paper towels. Continue with the remaining potatoes and batter.
3. Serve hot with Fresh Coconut and Mint Chutney (p. 15) or Fresh Mint Chutney (p. 17).

PER FRITTER:
   70 calories, 3g protein, 10g carbohydrates, 2g fat, 57mg sodium, 0mg cholesterol, 1.7g fiber

BELL PEPPER FRITTERS (SIMLA MIRCHI PAKORAS)

A zesty batter complements green or red bell peppers.

PREPARATION TIME: *15 minutes* COOKING TIME: *25 minutes* SERVES: 4 (MAKES 20 FRITTERS)

FOR THE BATTER:
1 cup chickpea flour (besan)
2 Tbsp. rice flour or rice powder
¼ tsp. garam masala (p. 25)
¼ tsp. chili powder
¼ tsp. ground cumin
1 Tbsp. fresh lime juice

½ tsp. salt
½ cup water
⅛ tsp. baking soda
3 bell peppers

Vegetable oil for deep-frying

1. Into a bowl, sift the chickpea flour and rice flour. Add the garam masala, chili powder, cumin, lime juice, and salt. Slowly add the water while beating the mixture with a wire whisk, until the batter has the consistency of heavy cream. Cover and set aside.

2. Seed and cut the bell peppers into long strips or into thick rounds.

3. In a wok or a deep-frying pan, heat the vegetable oil (about 3 inches deep) until the temperature reaches around 360 degrees.

4. Add the baking soda to the batter and beat for 1 minute.

5. Dip four or five bell pepper rings or strips into the batter, shake off the excess, and carefully lower them into the oil, one at a time. The oil temperature should be maintained at 325 degrees. Fry the pakoras for 3 to 4 minutes until they are golden brown on both sides. With a slotted spoon remove them and drain on paper towels. Fry the remaining peppers dipped in batter.

6. Serve hot with Fresh Cilantro Chutney (p. 17).

PER FRITTER:
68 calories, 3.5g protein, 9g carbohydrates, 2g fat, 45mg sodium, 0mg cholesterol, 1.5g fiber

BATTER-COATED SPICY MASHED POTATO BALLS (ALOO BONDAS)

Aloo bondas take a little longer to prepare than pakoras because they require several different steps, but you will find these absolutely delectable and well worth your time.

PREPARATION TIME: *30 minutes* COOKING TIME: *30 minutes* SERVES: 4 (MAKES 16 BONDAS)

FOR THE POTATO BALLS:
4 potatoes
1 Tbsp. vegetable oil
¼ tsp. ground turmeric
2 onions, peeled and finely chopped
1–2 green chilies or jalapeño
* peppers, chopped*
1 tsp. salt
2 Tbsp. lime juice
2 Tbsp. chopped fresh cilantro
¼ tsp. garam masala (p. 25)
* (optional)*

FOR THE BATTER:
1 cup chickpea flour (besan)
2 Tbsp. rice flour or rice powder
½ tsp. baking soda
¼ tsp. salt
¼ tsp. chili powder
½ cup water

Vegetable oil for deep-frying

To prepare the potato balls:
1. In a saucepan, with enough water to cover, boil the potatoes for 10 minutes until they are fork-tender, yet firm. Cool. Peel and dice them into ½-inch cubes.
2. In a nonstick saucepan, heat the oil. Add the turmeric, onions, and green chilies, and sauté over medium heat until the onions are soft. Remove from the heat. Add the potatoes, salt, lime juice, and cilantro (and garam masala, if desired). Stir until the potatoes are mashed and blended with the spices.

To prepare the batter:
3. Put all the batter ingredients in a bowl and slowly add the water, stirring constantly with a fork or wire whisk until the batter has the slightly thick consistency of cream.

To make the bondas:
4. Divide the potato mixture into 16 balls.
5. In a wok or a deep-frying pan, heat the oil (about 3 inches deep) until the temperature reaches 360 degrees. One at a time, dip a potato ball into the batter and coat it thoroughly, shaking off any excess. Carefully lower the ball into the oil. Fry four or five balls at a time for 3 to 4 minutes until they rise to the surface and are golden brown. The oil temperature should be maintained at 325 degrees. Remove

them with a slotted spoon and drain them on paper towels. Repeat the process with the remaining potato balls.

6. Serve hot with tomato sauce or any chutney of your choice.

PER BONDA:
  99 calories, 3g protein, 15g carbohydrates, 3g fat, 100mg sodium, 0mg cholesterol, 2.3g fiber

BREAD FRITTERS

PREPARATION TIME: *15 minutes* COOKING TIME: *25 minutes* SERVES: 4 (MAKES 20 FRITTERS)

8 slices home-style bread	¼ tsp. chili powder
½ cup low-fat plain yogurt	1–2 green chilies or jalapeño
½ cup water	peppers, minced
1 cup chickpea flour (besan)	2 Tbsp. chopped fresh cilantro
½ tsp. salt	
1 onion, peeled and chopped	Vegetable oil for deep-frying

1. Remove the crust from the bread and crumble. In a mixing bowl, dilute the yogurt with the water. Soak the bread pieces in the yogurt for 10 minutes.

2. Add the chickpea flour, salt, onion, chili powder, green chilies, and cilantro to the soaked bread. Mix well.

3. In a wok or a deep-frying pan, heat the oil (about 3 inches deep) until the temperature reaches 350 degrees. Carefully lower 6 to 8 tablespoonfuls of the bread mixture into the hot oil. Maintain the oil temperature at 325 degrees. Fry them until they turn golden brown. Remove with a slotted spoon and drain on paper towels.

4. Serve hot with Fresh Cilantro Chutney (page 17).

PER FRITTER:
  66 calories, 3g protein, 9g carbohydrates, 2g fat, 50mg sodium, 0.5mg cholesterol, 0.4g fiber

CHILI-CHEESE FRITTERS (MIRCHI BONDAS)

Cottage cheese blends well with bell peppers. Choose baby green bell peppers for this dish, available at specialty green markets.

PREPARATION TIME: *20 minutes* COOKING TIME: *25 minutes* SERVES: 4 (MAKES 16 FRITTERS)

8 ounces cottage cheese	*2 Tbsp. rice flour or rice powder*
1 onion, peeled and finely chopped	*½ tsp. salt*
½ tsp. salt	*1 tsp. baking soda*
16 baby bell peppers	*½ tsp. chili powder*
	1 cup water
FOR THE BATTER:	
1½ cups chickpea flour (besan)	*Vegetable oil for deep-frying*

1. In a bowl, mix the cottage cheese, onion, and salt, and set aside. Cut the tops off the peppers and scoop out the seeds. Blanch them in boiling, salted water for 1 minute and drain.
2. In a bowl, sift the chickpea flour and rice flour. Add salt, baking soda, and chili powder. Slowly add the water and beat with a fork or a wire whisk. The batter should have the consistency of pancake batter.
3. Stuff the peppers with the cheese mixture.
4. In a wok or a deep-frying pan, heat the oil (about 3 inches deep) until the temperature reaches 350 degrees. Dip the stuffed peppers in the batter and carefully lower them, one at a time, into the hot oil and fry them until golden brown. Maintain the oil temperature at 325 degrees. Remove them with a slotted spoon and drain them on paper towels.
5. Serve hot with any fresh chutney (see Chapter 1) or tomato sauce.

PER FRITTER:
102 calories, 5g protein, 16g carbohydrates, 2g fat, 100mg sodium, 2mg cholesterol, 3.5g fiber

CHAPTER 3

SOUPS

....

VEGETABLE BROTH

SPICY TOMATO SOUP

CAULIFLOWER AND POTATO SOUP

ASPARAGUS SOUP

COLD CUCUMBER SOUP

MUSHROOM SOUP

SPICY GREEN PEA SOUP

CREAM OF SPINACH SOUP

CORN SOUP

CHILI BEAN SOUP

MULLIGATAWNY SOUP

SPICY LENTIL BROTH

RED LENTIL SOUP

SPICY POTATO SOUP

GARDEN VEGETABLE SOUP

SPLIT PEA AND SPINACH SOUP

SOUPS

*T*hese soups range from the simple and delicate to the more complex and hearty. The biggest advantage of soups is that they can be prepared well in advance and frozen. Defrost and reheat just before serving.

In many cases, I have provided instructions for both microwave and conventional cooking methods.

....

VEGETABLE BROTH

*O*ne of the most important ingredients for soups is the broth. Below I have given you a list of suggested ingredients, but you may add any other vegetables that are available, such as pea pods, zucchini, green pepper, and so on.

MAKES 4 CUPS

6–7 cups water
2 red onions, peeled and quartered
2 potatoes, peeled and diced
2 large ripe tomatoes, halved
1 celery stalk, halved

1 clove garlic, minced (optional)
2 black peppercorns
1 bay leaf
6 fresh cilantro stems
Salt to taste

1. Stove-top Method: In a large saucepan or stockpot, bring the water to a boil and add all the ingredients. Simmer over low heat for 25 to 30 minutes. Off the heat, steep for 5 minutes. Pour the mixture through a fine-meshed strainer and discard the vegetables.

OR

Microwave Method: In a 3-quart microwave-safe bowl, combine all the ingredients. Cook on high (100%) for 10 minutes. Stir once. Cook for another 10 minutes.

Let the broth steep for 5 minutes. Pour the liquid through a fine-meshed strainer and discard the vegetables.

2. This broth can be stored in the refrigerator for 4 days. When cooled, it can also be frozen for up to 1 month.

SPICY TOMATO SOUP

*S*easoned with mild spices, this smooth soup is easy to prepare and appealing year round, served either hot or chilled.

PREPARATION TIME: *10 minutes* COOKING TIME: *25 minutes* SERVES: 4

3 *cups vegetable broth or water*	⅛ *tsp. cayenne pepper*
3 *ripe tomatoes (about 1 pound) or*	⅛ *tsp. ground cloves*
whole canned Italian plum	½ *tsp. salt*
tomatoes, drained	1 *tsp. fresh lemon juice*
1 *onion, finely chopped*	
1 *clove garlic, minced*	FOR GARNISH:
⅛ *tsp. ground cumin*	½ *cup low-fat plain yogurt*
⅛ *tsp. freshly ground black pepper*	1 *Tbsp. chopped fresh cilantro*

1. Stove-top Method: In a 3-quart saucepan, bring the vegetable broth to a boil. Add the tomatoes, onion, garlic, cumin, black pepper, cayenne pepper, cloves, salt, and lemon juice. Simmer for 10 to 15 minutes. Off the heat, let the soup stand for 5 minutes.

OR

Microwave Method: In a microwave-safe bowl, combine the vegetable broth, tomatoes, onion, garlic, cumin, black pepper, cayenne pepper, cloves, salt, and lemon juice. Cook covered on high (100%) for 6 minutes. Stir the contents and cook on high for another 6 to 8 minutes. Let stand for 5 minutes.

For both methods, follow steps 2 and 3 below:

2. In a food processor fitted with a metal blade or in a blender, process the mixture to a fine puree. Pour the mixture into a saucepan, bring to a boil, reduce the heat to low, and allow the soup to simmer for 5 minutes.

3. Garnish with a spoonful of yogurt and chopped cilantro.

PER SERVING:
   58 calories, 3g protein, 7g carbohydrates, 2g fat, 236mg sodium, 2.5mg cholesterol, 2g fiber

CAULIFLOWER AND POTATO SOUP

This combination of vegetables adds a delicate flavor to this substantial creamy soup.

PREPARATION TIME: *10 minutes* COOKING TIME: *20 minutes* SERVES: 4

1 small head cauliflower	*¼ tsp. freshly ground black pepper*
2 onions	*¼ tsp. salt or to taste*
2 small potatoes	*2 cups skim or 1% milk*
3 cups vegetable broth or water	
1–2 jalapeño peppers, according to	GARNISH:
taste, stemmed	*2 Tbsp. chopped fresh cilantro*

1. Cut the cauliflower into florets. Peel and cube the onions and the potatoes.

2. Stove-top Method: In a large saucepan, combine the broth, cauliflower, onions, potatoes, and jalapeño peppers. Bring to a boil, then reduce the heat and simmer for 6 to 8 minutes until the vegetables are tender, but still have texture.

OR

Microwave Method: In a large microwave-safe bowl, combine only 1 cup broth, the cauliflower, onions, potatoes, and jalapeño peppers. Cook on high (100%) for 8 to 10 minutes, until the vegetables are tender but still have texture.

For both methods, follow steps 3 and 4 below:

3. Reserve a handful of florets to garnish. In a food processor fitted with a steel blade or a blender, process the mixture to a puree. Strain the puree into the saucepan. Add black pepper, salt, and milk to the soup. Bring to a boil, then reduce the heat and simmer for 5 minutes.

4. Garnish with the reserved florets and chopped cilantro.

PER SERVING:

150 calories, 9g protein, 23g carbohydrates, 2.5g fat, 296mg sodium, 5mg cholesterol, 2.5g fiber

ASPARAGUS SOUP

If you like asparagus, you will love this mildly spiced soup. The creamy yogurt cheese lends a tangy flavor.

PREPARATION TIME: *5 minutes* COOKING TIME: *20 minutes* SERVES: 4

2 cups vegetable broth or water	⅛ tsp. garam masala (p. 25)
½ lb. asparagus, cleaned, tough	⅛ tsp. curry powder
ends discarded, and cut into	⅛ tsp. salt
2-inch pieces	
1 onion, peeled and diced	GARNISH:
2 potatoes, peeled and diced	1 cup yogurt cheese (p. 10)
1 cup skim or 1% milk	

1. Stove-top Method: In a saucepan, bring the vegetable broth to a boil. Add the asparagus, onion, and potatoes, and simmer for 10 to 15 minutes, until they are tender.

OR

Microwave Method: In a 3-quart microwave-safe bowl, combine only 1 cup vegetable broth with the asparagus, onion, and potatoes. Cook on high (100%) for 5 minutes. Stir once and cook for 5 minutes more, until the vegetables are tender.

For both methods, follow steps 2 and 3 below:

2. In a food processor fitted with a steel blade or a blender, puree the mixture. Pour the mixture into a saucepan and add the milk, garam masala, curry powder, and salt. Simmer for 5 minutes.

3. Garnish with a dollop of yogurt cheese. This soup can be served either hot or cold.

PER SERVING:
   159 calories, 10g protein, 23g carbohydrates, 3g fat, 206mg sodium, 8mg cholesterol, 2.2g fiber

COLD CUCUMBER SOUP

his cool soup is ideal for a hot summer day.

PREPARATION TIME: *5 minutes* COOKING TIME: *10 minutes* SERVES: 4

3 cups water
5 cucumbers, peeled, seeded, and
   cut into chunks
1 cup skim milk
2 cups low-fat plain yogurt
1–2 jalapeño peppers, stemmed, to
   taste
2–4 fresh mint leaves
2 tsp. light vegetable oil

1 tsp. cumin seeds
1 green bell pepper, seeded and
   chopped
¼ tsp. salt, or to taste

GARNISH:
2 Tbsp. chopped fresh cilantro or
   parsley

1. In a saucepan, boil the water and add the cucumbers. Reduce the heat and simmer for 5 minutes, until the cucumbers are soft. Drain.

2. In a blender or a food processor fitted with a steel blade, puree the cucumbers, milk, yogurt, jalapeño peppers, and mint leaves. Set aside.

3. In a saucepan, heat the oil. Sauté the cumin seeds and bell pepper for 1 minute. Add the cucumber puree and salt, and simmer for 2 minutes. (Be careful not to boil the soup, which will cause the yogurt to separate.) Chill.

4. Garnish with chopped cilantro or parsley.

PER SERVING:

147 calories, 10g protein, 17g carbohydrates, 4g fat, 220mg sodium, 12mg cholesterol, 2.9g fiber

MUSHROOM SOUP

This high-protein, versatile soup can be served with rice, pasta, or vegetable dishes.

PREPARATION TIME: *10 minutes* COOKING TIME: *10 minutes* SERVES: 4

1 Tbsp. light vegetable oil or olive oil
1 lb. fresh button mushrooms, chopped
1 potato, peeled and diced
1 onion, peeled and diced
2 cups vegetable broth

½ tsp. chili powder
¼ tsp. ground cumin
¼ tsp. freshly ground black pepper
Salt to taste

GARNISH:
4 Tbsp. yogurt cheese (p. 10)

1. In a nonstick 3-quart saucepan, heat the oil. Sauté the mushrooms, potato, and onion for 3 to 4 minutes. Add the vegetable broth; bring to a boil, then simmer for 8 minutes, until the vegetables are tender.
2. In a food processor fitted with a steel blade, or a blender, puree the mixture and return it to the saucepan. Add the chili powder, cumin, pepper, and salt, and bring the soup back to a boil.
3. Serve hot with a tablespoon of yogurt cheese.

PER SERVING:

114 calories, 5g protein, 12g carbohydrates, 4g fat, 243mg sodium, 1.2mg cholesterol, 0.7g fiber

SPICY GREEN PEA SOUP

This soup tastes best with sweet peas in season. Double the quantity, freeze it, and you can have this garden-fresh taste any time of the year.

PREPARATION TIME: *15 minutes* COOKING TIME: *25 minutes* SERVES: 4

1 Tbsp. extra-virgin olive oil
1 medium onion, peeled and thinly
  sliced
2 lbs. fresh green peas, shelled
½ tsp. curry powder
½ tsp. ground cumin
½ tsp. freshly ground black pepper

3 cups vegetable broth
1 tsp. salt or to taste
2 Tbsp. lime juice

GARNISH:
¼ cup low-fat plain yogurt
2 Tbsp. chopped fresh cilantro

1. Stove-top Method: In a 3-quart saucepan, heat the oil. Add the onion and sauté for 2 minutes. Add the peas, curry powder, cumin, pepper, and vegetable broth; bring to a boil. Reduce the heat and simmer for 15 minutes, until the peas are tender.

OR

Microwave Method: In a microwave-safe 3-quart bowl, combine the olive oil and onion, and cook on high (100%) for 45 seconds. Add the peas, curry powder, cumin, black pepper, and ½ cup vegetable broth. Cook, covered, on high for 4 minutes; stir and cook another 4 minutes, until peas are tender. Add the remaining broth.

For both methods, follow steps 2 and 3 below:
2. In a blender or food processor fitted with a steel blade, puree the mixture. Transfer the puree to a saucepan. Add the salt and lime juice, and simmer for 5 minutes.
3. Serve hot or at room temperature with a tablespoon of the yogurt and cilantro.

PER SERVING:
  100 calories, 5g protein, 11g carbohydrates, 4g fat, 258mg sodium, 2mg cholesterol, 2.4g fiber

CREAM OF SPINACH SOUP

Spinach takes on a whole new dimension in this subtly spiced soup.

PREPARATION TIME: *10 minutes* COOKING TIME: *20 minutes* SERVES: *4*

1 Tbsp. light vegetable oil
1 onion, peeled and chopped
1 lb. fresh spinach, thoroughly
   washed, stemmed, and chopped,
   or 1 (10 oz.) package frozen
   chopped spinach, thawed
2 cups vegetable broth
1 cup skim or 1% milk

⅛ tsp. cayenne pepper
¼ tsp. curry powder
Pinch ground nutmeg
½ Tbsp. fresh lime juice
¼ tsp. salt

GARNISH:
½ cup low-fat plain yogurt

1. Stove-top Method: In a saucepan, heat the oil over medium heat. Add the onion and sauté for 2 minutes. Add the spinach and vegetable broth. Bring to a boil. Reduce the heat and simmer for 8 to 10 minutes, until the spinach is tender. Cool.

OR

Microwave Method: In a microwave-safe bowl, combine the oil and onion. Cook on high (100%) for 1 minute. Add the spinach and only ½ cup of vegetable broth and cook, covered, on high for 5 to 7 minutes, until the spinach is tender. Add the remaining broth. Cool.

For both methods, follow step 2 below:

2. In a food processor fitted with a steel blade, or a blender, puree the mixture. Pour the puree into a saucepan. Add the remaining ingredients except the yogurt and simmer for 5 minutes, until the soup is heated through. Serve hot garnished with a swirl of yogurt in each bowl.

PER SERVING:
   118 caloriess, 7g protein, 11g carbohydrates, 5g fat, 228mg sodium, 5mg cholesterol, 2.4g fiber

CORN SOUP

⁂

*C*urry powder imparts a zesty flavor to this hearty soup.

PREPARATION TIME: *15 minutes* COOKING TIME: *35 minutes* SERVES: 4

2 Tbsp. light vegetable oil
2 onions, peeled and chopped
2 jalapeño peppers, seeded and
   chopped
2 potatoes, peeled and diced
Kernels from 2 ears of corn, or 1
   (17 oz.) can whole corn
2 cups water

½ tsp. curry powder
½ tsp. cayenne pepper
½ tsp. salt or to taste
1½ cups skim or 1% milk

GARNISH:
2 Tbsp. chopped fresh cilantro

1. Stove-top Method: In a heavy-bottomed nonstick saucepan, heat the oil over medium heat. Add the onions and jalapeño peppers. Sauté for 2 minutes. Add the potatoes, corn, and water. Bring to a boil. Reduce the heat and simmer for 20 to 25 minutes, or until corn is tender but not mushy. If you are using canned corn, simmer for 15 minutes.

OR

Microwave Method: In a microwave-safe bowl, combine the oil, onions, and jalapeño peppers. Cook on high (100%) for 45 seconds. Add the potatoes, corn, and only 1 cup of water. If it is fresh corn, cook for 6 to 8 minutes; if the corn is from a can, cook on high for 4 to 6 minutes. Stir and cook on high for 3 more minutes, until the corn is tender but not mushy. Add the remaining cup of water.

For both methods, follow steps 2 and 3 below:
2. In a food processor fitted with a steel blade, or a blender, process the mixture to a coarse puree. Put the contents into a saucepan. Add the curry powder, cayenne pepper, salt, and milk. Bring the soup just up to a boil, lower the heat, and simmer for 5 minutes.
3. Garnish with cilantro. This soup can be served hot or cold.

PER SERVING:

180 calories, 5g protein, 22g carbohydrates, 8g fat, 265mg sodium, 4mg cholesterol, 4g fiber

CHILI BEAN SOUP

This hearty bean soup serves as a meal all on its own. If you have the time, use dried kidney beans (see cooking instructions on page *159*). Canned beans are a reasonably good substitute. Chili sauce is available in specialty markets.

PREPARATION TIME: *10 minutes* COOKING TIME: *25 minutes* SERVES: 4

2 Tbsp. light vegetable oil
2 onions, peeled and thinly sliced
2 cloves garlic, minced
2 green bell peppers, seeded and
    finely chopped
2 scallions, sliced
1 cup tomato puree
1 (16 oz.) can kidney beans, or
    1 cup dried kidney beans,
    presoaked and cooked

⅛ tsp. chili sauce
1 tsp. sugar
1 cup vegetable broth
½ tsp. salt
2 ripe tomatoes, chopped

1 Tbsp. freshly grated Parmesan
    cheese

In a 3-quart nonstick saucepan, heat the oil. Add the onions, garlic, bell peppers, and scallions. Sauté for 4 minutes, until tender. Add the tomato puree, kidney beans, chili sauce, sugar, vegetable broth, and salt, and simmer over medium-low heat for 15 minutes. Add the chopped tomatoes and simmer for an additional 2 minutes. Sprinkle with grated Parmesan cheese. Serve hot.

PER SERVING:

235 calories, 10g protein, 31g carbohydrates, 8g fat, 295mg sodium, 1mg cholesterol, 8.5g fiber

MULLIGATAWNY SOUP (MULLAGATANNI SOUP)

This delicious soup is one of my favorites because the coconut milk lends a sweet, creamy taste. Any commercial brand of curry powder can be used in this soup to get authentic results.

PREPARATION TIME: *10 minutes* COOKING TIME: *45 minutes* SERVES: 4

½ cup toovar dal or dried yellow
   split peas
2 Tbsp. light vegetable oil
2 onions, peeled and chopped
2 cloves garlic, peeled and minced
½ inch fresh ginger, peeled and
   grated
¼ tsp. ground turmeric
1 carrot, peeled and chopped
5 cups water

2 ripe tomatoes, cored and
   chopped
1–2 tsp. curry powder
¼ tsp. freshly ground black pepper
½ cup thick coconut milk or ½ cup
   half-and-half
Salt to taste
2 Tbsp. finely chopped fresh
   cilantro

1. In a fine sieve, pick over the dal and rinse thoroughly.
2. In a 3-quart saucepan, heat the oil. Add the onions, garlic, ginger, turmeric, and carrot, and sauté for 2 to 3 minutes. Add the dal, water, chopped tomatoes, curry powder, and pepper. Simmer over medium heat for 35 minutes, until the split peas are soft. Cool.
3. In a food processor fitted with a steel blade, or a blender, puree the split pea mixture. Strain the soup through a sieve into the saucepan. Add the coconut milk, salt, and cilantro. Gently simmer for 5 minutes. Serve hot.

PER SERVING:
   205 calories, 7g protein, 19g carbohydrates, 11g fat, 240mg sodium, 15mg cholesterol, 7g fiber

SPICY LENTIL BROTH (MYSORE RASAM)

Rasam literally means "broth" in Sanskrit. This soup is traditionally made with lentils, toovar or arhar dal, to give the broth a creamy, thick texture. The lentil broth is highly seasoned with spices, tamarind water, and ripe tomatoes. It is one of India's most popular soups. If you are not able to get toovar dal, you can substitute dried yellow split peas, which you can find in any supermarket. If you do not have tamarind paste, just use more tomatoes and two tablespoons of lime juice. With these substitutions, the soup may not be as authentic, but it will still be full of flavor.

PREPARATION TIME: *10 minutes* COOKING TIME: *45 minutes* SERVES: 4

½ cup toovar dal or dried yellow
    split peas
5 cups water
¼ tsp. ground turmeric
½ inch fresh ginger, peeled and
    grated
2 ripe tomatoes, cored and chopped
½ tsp. cayenne pepper
¼ tsp. freshly ground black pepper
¼ tsp. ground cumin
½ tsp. ground coriander

½ tsp. brown sugar
2 tsp. tamarind paste or 2 Tbsp.
    fresh lime juice
½ tsp. salt or to taste

FOR SEASONING:
2 tsp. light vegetable oil
½ tsp. black mustard seeds
⅛ tsp. ground asafetida

2 Tbsp. chopped fresh cilantro

1. In a sieve, pick over the dal and rinse thoroughly. In a 3-quart saucepan, combine the water, dal, turmeric, and ginger. Bring to a boil. Reduce the heat to medium and simmer for 30 to 35 minutes, until the dal is tender. As it cools, a thick layer of broth will collect on the top. Carefully skim this broth into another saucepan. To the broth add the tomatoes, cayenne pepper, black pepper, cumin, coriander, sugar, tamarind paste, and salt. Simmer over medium heat for 5 minutes.
2. For seasoning: In a small saucepan over medium heat, heat the oil. Add the mustard seeds and cover until you hear the seeds pop and sputter. Add the asafetida and turn off the heat. Add the contents of this pan to the broth.
3. Garnish with cilantro and serve hot. The cooked dal can be reserved for use in any vegetable curry or as an accompaniment for plain rice.

PER SERVING:
> 145 calories, 5g protein, 15g carbohydrates, 7g fat, 222mg sodium, 0mg cholesterol, 5g fiber

RED LENTIL SOUP

*R*ed lentils don't need presoaking and take approximately 20 to 25 minutes to cook. If you like your soup spicy, add the jalapeño peppers.

PREPARATION TIME: *10 minutes* COOKING TIME: *35 minutes* SERVES: 4

1 cup split red lentils
5 cups vegetable broth or water
⅛ tsp. ground turmeric
1 onion, peeled and finely chopped
2 hot peppers or jalapeño peppers, stemmed (optional)
2 carrots, peeled and diced
1 potato, peeled and diced
½ tsp. cayenne pepper
½ tsp. curry powder
2 Tbsp. fresh lime or lemon juice
½ tsp. salt or to taste

FOR SEASONING:
2 tsp. vegetable or olive oil
½ tsp. cumin seeds
⅛ tsp. ground asafetida

GARNISH:
4 Tbsp. plain yogurt or yogurt cheese (p. 10)
2 Tbsp. chopped fresh cilantro or parsley

1. In a sieve, pick over and rinse the lentils thoroughly.
2. In a 4-quart saucepan, bring the broth to a boil and add the lentils and turmeric. Reduce the heat to medium. After 10 minutes, add the onion (and jalapeño peppers, if desired), carrots, and potato, and simmer for 20 minutes, until the lentils and vegetables are tender. Let cool slightly. Transfer the contents of the saucepan to a blender or a food processor fitted with a steel blade and process to a coarse puree.
3. Pour the puree back into the saucepan. Add the cayenne pepper, curry powder, lime juice, and salt, and simmer gently for 5 minutes.

4. For the seasoning: In a small saucepan, heat the oil. Add the cumin seeds and asafetida. When the contents of the pan start to sizzle, remove the pan from the heat. Stir seasonings into the soup.

5. Serve hot with a tablespoon of yogurt or yogurt cheese and cilantro.

PER SERVING:

125 calories, 7g protein, 22g carbohydrates, 1g fat, 250mg sodium, 1.7mg cholesterol, 6g fiber

SPICY POTATO SOUP

*T*his zippy soup is light and fairly smooth with a medium consistency.

PREPARATION TIME: *10 minutes* COOKING TIME: *35 minutes* SERVES: 4

1 Tbsp. light vegetable oil
1 onion, peeled and chopped
3 potatoes, peeled and cut into
  1-inch cubes
3 cups vegetable broth or water

FOR THE SPICE BAG, IN A PIECE OF
CHEESECLOTH TIE:
½ tsp. black peppercorns

3 whole cloves
2-inch cinnamon stick, broken into
  2 pieces
1 green cardamom pod

½ tsp. salt
2 Tbsp. chopped fresh cilantro
½ cup whole, low-fat, or skim milk

1. In a nonstick 3-quart saucepan, heat the oil. Add the onion and potatoes, and sauté over medium heat for 8 to 10 minutes, until the onion is limp and turns golden. Add the broth and spice bag, and bring to a boil. Reduce the heat and simmer for 15 minutes, until the vegetables are tender. Remove from the heat, add the salt and cilantro, and let cool.

2. When the mixture is cool, discard the spice bag, squeezing the liquid back into the soup. Transfer the contents of the saucepan into a blender or a food processor fitted with a steel blade and puree the soup.

3. Return the soup to the saucepan and bring to a boil. Turn down the heat, add the milk, and simmer for 2 minutes. Serve hot.

PER SERVING:

122 calories, 4g protein, 16g carbohydrates, 4.5g fat, 250mg sodium, 4mg cholesterol, 2.5g fiber

GARDEN VEGETABLE SOUP

I have suggested vegetable ingredients below, but you can use any vegetables to prepare this soup: parsnip, cauliflower, carrots, peas, pearl onions, zucchini, celery, fennel, and so on, to fit the season and your palate.

PREPARATION TIME: *15 minutes* COOKING TIME: *30 minutes* SERVES: 4

1 Tbsp. olive oil or vegetable oil
1 red onion, peeled and chopped
2 cloves garlic, peeled and minced
2 chili peppers or jalapeño peppers, seeded and minced (optional)
3 carrots, peeled and diced
1 green or red bell pepper, seeded and diced
1 large potato, peeled and diced
½ cup fresh peas or thawed frozen peas
4 cups vegetable broth or water

1 Tbsp. tomato paste
½ tsp. cayenne pepper
½ tsp. ground cumin
½ tsp. ground coriander
¼ tsp. garam masala (p. 25) (optional)
½ tsp. brown sugar
½ tsp. salt or to taste

GARNISH:
1 Tbsp. chopped fresh cilantro

1. In a 3-quart nonstick saucepan, heat the oil. Add the onion and garlic (and chili peppers, if desired), and sauté over medium heat for 5 minutes. Add the carrots, bell peppers, potato, and peas, and sauté for 5 minutes more. Add the vegetable broth and simmer over medium heat for 15 to 20 minutes, until the vegetables are tender.

2. Stir in the tomato paste, cayenne pepper, cumin, coriander (and garam masala, if desired), brown sugar, and salt, and bring to a boil. Garnish with cilantro and serve hot with toast or whole wheat pita bread.

PER SERVING:
> 98 calories, 2g protein, 12g carbohydrates, 4.5g fat, 154mg sodium, 0mg cholesterol, 3g fiber

SPLIT PEA AND SPINACH SOUP

*T*he fragrant mix of spices lends a flavorful spark to this split pea and spinach combo.

PREPARATION TIME: *10 minutes* COOKING TIME: *45 minutes* SERVES: 4

½ cup toovar dal or yellow split peas
4 cups water
¼ tsp. ground turmeric
1 lb. fresh spinach, thoroughly washed, stemmed, and chopped, or 1 (10 oz.) package thawed frozen chopped spinach
1 onion, peeled and chopped

2 cloves garlic, peeled and diced
2 green chilies or jalapeño peppers, stemmed
½ tsp. ground cumin
½ tsp. ground coriander
½ tsp. chili powder
½ tsp. curry powder
½ tsp. salt
½ cup whole, low-fat, or skim milk

1. In a sieve, pick over dal and rinse thoroughly.
2. In a 3-quart saucepan, bring the water to a boil. Add the toovar dal and turmeric, and reduce the heat to medium. Simmer for 25 minutes. Add the spinach, onion, garlic, and chilies, and continue to simmer for another 15 minutes until the peas are tender. Add the cumin, coriander, chili powder, curry powder, and salt, and simmer for 5 more minutes. Cool.
3. Transfer the contents of the saucepan to a blender or a food processor fitted with a steel blade, and puree.
4. Return the soup to the saucepan. Add the milk and simmer for 5 minutes to heat through. Serve hot.

PER SERVING:
> 105 calories, 8g protein, 15g carbohydrates, 2g fat, 284mg sodium, 4mg cholesterol, 7g fiber

CHAPTER 4

SALADS

....

SALADS

$\mathscr{A}$ salad can be so much more than just lettuce and tomato. Some of these salads may surprise you. As is traditional in my native India, I love combining the sweet with the savory, the spicy with the mild—and that preference is reflected in these recipes. Please note that many of these recipes call for jalapeño or chili peppers, red pepper flakes, or hot pepper sauce. Use them judiciously until you get accustomed to the spicy flavors of India. Please see my note on page 13 on handling hot peppers.

Use tomato or cucumber slices for everyday garnishes, but for added color and flair, try radish roses, celery or cucumber curls, or onion or bell pepper rings.

To make radish roses: Use a radish press to create the petals. If you do not have a press, trim the top and the root end with a sharp knife, and cut an X into the radish halfway through from the top. Turn the radish at an angle, cut another X so that now you have 8 equal sections. Chill in ice water for 10 minutes until they open up.

....

CARROT AND GREEN BELL PEPPER SALAD

$\mathscr{C}$arrots give a touch of sweetness to this crunchy and colorful salad.

PREPARATION TIME: *10 minutes* NO COOKING SERVES: 4

4 carrots, peeled, trimmed, and
   finely chopped
2 green bell peppers, seeded and
   finely chopped
2 Tbsp. fresh lime juice

½ tsp. salt or to taste
2 green chilies or jalapeño peppers,
   minced
2 Tbsp. chopped fresh cilantro

In a bowl, combine all the ingredients and stir. Refrigerate for 2 hours before serving.

PER SERVING:
> 45 calories, 1g protein, 9g carbohydrates, 0.8g fat, 240mg sodium, 0mg cholesterol, 3g fiber

FRUIT SALAD WITH YOGURT CHEESE DRESSING

A perfect salad for a hot summer day. You can substitute your favorite fruits for those listed below. Yogurt cheese is a perfect low-fat replacement for sour cream or mayonnaise in this bright and refreshing salad.

PREPARATION TIME: *15 minutes* NO COOKING SERVES: 4

FOR THE FRUIT SALAD:
- 3 mandarin oranges, peeled and sectioned
- ½ fresh pineapple, rind removed, cored and cut into chunks
- 1 apple, peeled, cored and diced
- 1 cup seedless red or green grapes

FOR THE YOGURT CHEESE DRESSING:
- 1 cup yogurt cheese (p. 10)
- 2 tsp. lemon juice
- 2 tsp. honey
- ¼ tsp. paprika
- ¼ tsp. Tabasco sauce
- ¼ tsp. salt
- 2 Tbsp. chopped fresh cilantro or parsley

In a bowl, combine the fruit salad ingredients and stir. In a separate bowl, combine all the dressing ingredients and beat with a wire whisk until smooth. Fold the dressing into the fruit. Chill for 1 hour and serve.

PER SERVING:
> 200 calories, 5.5g protein, 39g carbohydrates, 2.5g fat, 170mg sodium, 5mg cholesterol, 2g fiber

HOT FRUIT SALAD

❧

I like to serve this salad to complement the hot spiciness of the vegetable curries and rice dishes. Also, when fresh fruit is out of season, this is the perfect salad. You can use canned fruits packed in light syrup.

PREPARATION TIME: *15 minutes* COOKING TIME: *5 minutes* SERVES: 4

1 (8 oz.) can mandarin oranges
1 (8 oz.) can pineapple chunks
1 (8 oz.) can peaches
2 ripe bananas, peeled and
  quartered

2 Tbsp. brown sugar
½ tsp. ground cinnamon

1. Drain the oranges, pineapple, and peaches, reserving ½ cup of syrup. Set aside.
2. Stove-top Method: In a 3-quart saucepan, add the oranges, pineapple, peaches, and bananas. Sprinkle the brown sugar, cinnamon, and the reserved syrup on top and heat it for 5 to 7 minutes. Serve hot.

OR

Microwave Method: Arrange the oranges, pineapple, peaches, and bananas on a microwave-safe dish. Sprinkle the brown sugar, cinnamon, and the reserved syrup on top and heat in a microwave oven on high (100%) for 5 minutes. Serve hot.

PER SERVING:
  175 calories, 1.5g protein, 40g carbohydrates, 1g fat, 17mg sodium, 0mg cholesterol, 1g fiber

CHICKPEA AND RICE SALAD

❧

*R*ed onion adds spark to the nutty flavor of chickpeas.

PREPARATION TIME: *20 minutes* COOKING TIME: *20 minutes* SERVES: 4

1 Tbsp. extra-virgin olive oil
1 red onion, peeled, sliced, and
  separated into rings
1 green bell pepper, seeded and
  chopped
2 chilies or jalapeño peppers,
  seeded and chopped
2 ripe tomatoes, cored and
  chopped

Salt to taste
1 Tbsp. fresh lime juice
Lettuce leaves
1 (10 oz.) can chickpeas, drained
  and rinsed
1 cup long-grain rice, cooked

GARNISH:
½ cup low-fat plain yogurt

1. In a nonstick saucepan, heat the oil. Add the onion, bell pepper, and chilies. Sauté over high heat until the onion rings are soft. Add the tomatoes, salt, and lime juice, and stir. Set aside.

2. On a large serving platter arrange the lettuce leaves. Spoon the chickpeas and then the rice over the lettuce. Spread the sautéed vegetable mixture on top. Garnish with yogurt and serve at room temperature.

PER SERVING:
  313 calories, 9g protein, 52g carbohydrates, 7g fat, 233mg sodium, 2.5mg cholesterol, 8g fiber

SPICED RICE SALAD

Ginger and cayenne pepper give this colorful, invigorating salad a unique flavor and texture.

PREPARATION TIME: *15 minutes* COOKING TIME: *30 minutes* SERVES: *4*

1 cup uncooked long-grain or
basmati rice
1 Tbsp. olive oil or light vegetable
oil
2 red onions, peeled and chopped
1 red bell pepper, seeded and finely
chopped
1–2 jalapeño peppers, finely
chopped
1 inch fresh ginger, peeled and
grated

½ cup fresh or thawed frozen peas
¼–½ tsp. cayenne pepper
¼ tsp. crushed red pepper
2 Tbsp. fresh lime juice
½ cup fresh or drained canned
pineapple chunks
Salt to taste
2 Tbsp. chopped fresh cilantro

1. Rinse and cook the rice according to your favorite method. Cool.
2. In a nonstick skillet or saucepan over medium-high heat, heat the oil. Add
onions, bell pepper, jalapeño peppers, ginger, and peas. Sauté for 10 minutes, until
the vegetables are tender but still crisp. Add the cayenne pepper, crushed red pepper, lime juice, pineapple chunks, and salt, and stir well.
3. Mix the rice and vegetables together. Garnish with chopped cilantro. Serve.

PER SERVING:
199 calories, 4g protein, 38g carbohydrates, 3.5g fat, 215mg sodium, 0mg
cholesterol, 2.5g fiber

PINEAPPLE, CUCUMBER, AND BEET SALAD

This tangy, sweet salad is suitable for both winter and summer menus. Garnish
with the beet slices just before serving; otherwise the beets may bleed into the salad.

PREPARATION TIME: 15 minutes COOKING TIME: 20 minutes SERVES: 4

½ fresh pineapple, cored, rind
   removed, and cut into chunks
2 cucumbers, peeled, seeded, and
   cut into ¼-inch-thick, 1-inch-long
   chunks
2 potatoes, boiled and diced

FOR THE SALAD DRESSING:
1 cup low-fat plain yogurt

½ tsp. cayenne pepper
¼ tsp. salt
1 tsp. honey
1 Tbsp. fresh lime juice
1 Tbsp. vegetable oil

Lettuce leaves
1 beet, boiled, skinned, and thinly
   sliced

1. In a large bowl, combine the pineapple, cucumbers, and potatoes.

2. In a small bowl, combine the yogurt, cayenne pepper, salt, honey, lime juice, and vegetable oil. Beat with a wire whisk until smooth. Drizzle the dressing over the salad and stir. Chill thoroughly.

3. On a platter, arrange the lettuce leaves. Spoon the salad over the leaves, garnish with the beet slices, and serve.

PER SERVING:
   160 calories, 5g protein, 26g carbohydrates, 4g fat, 289mg sodium, 5mg cholesterol, 2g fiber

SPICY CHICKPEA AND POTATO SALAD

Combine your favorite vegetables to create a salad to suit your taste. Experiment with different combinations such as kidney beans and kohlrabi or chayote squash (also known as mirlitons or vegetable pears).

PREPARATION TIME: *10 minutes* COOKING TIME: *20 minutes* SERVES: *4*

5 cups water

4 potatoes, approximately 1½ lbs.,
   peeled and cubed

FOR THE DRESSING:
1 cup low-fat plain yogurt
2 tsp. freshly ground black pepper
¼ tsp. salt
¼–½ tsp. curry powder, according
   to taste

1 Tbsp. fresh lime juice
4 scallions, finely chopped

1 (19 oz.) can chickpeas, drained
   and rinsed

GARNISH:
1 ripe tomato, thinly sliced
2 Tbsp. finely chopped fresh
   parsley or cilantro

1. In a 3-quart saucepan bring the water to a boil. Add the potatoes and simmer for about 15 minutes, until they are tender but still firm. Drain.

2. In a large bowl, whisk together the yogurt, pepper, salt, curry powder, lime juice, and scallions. While the potatoes are still warm, add them to the bowl. Stir in the chickpeas and serve garnished with the tomato slices and parsley.

PER SERVING:
   193 calories, 9g protein, 32g carbohydrates, 3g fat, 264mg sodium, 5mg cholesterol, 8.5g fiber

MIXED BEAN SALAD

I've used canned beans in this scrumptious-tasting salad, but of course, if you have the time, please use dried beans that are presoaked and cooked (see instructions on p. 159). They add a wonderful depth and dimension to the salad.

PREPARATION TIME: *10 minutes* COOKING TIME: *10 minutes* SERVES: 4

1 (19 oz.) can chickpeas
1 (16 oz.) can red kidney beans
1½ cups fresh peas or 1 (10 oz.)
    package frozen peas

FOR GARNISH:
1 Tbsp. olive or vegetable oil
1 red onion, peeled and cut into
    thin rings
1 green bell pepper, seeded and cut
    into thin rings

FOR THE DRESSING:
1 Tbsp. olive or vegetable oil
1 Tbsp. fresh lime juice
1 Tbsp. orange juice
1 tsp. oregano
¼ tsp. hot pepper sauce
¼ tsp. cayenne pepper
¼ tsp. salt

1. In a sieve, drain the chickpeas and kidney beans and rinse thoroughly with cold water.
2. In boiling water, cook the peas for 10 minutes or until done. Drain and set aside.
3. In a skillet, heat the oil. Add the onion rings and bell pepper, and sauté until they are tender but still crisp, about 3 minutes. Drain on paper towel.
4. In a salad bowl, combine the chickpeas, kidney beans, and peas. In a separate bowl, combine all the dressing ingredients and add to the peas and beans. Stir. Garnish with the onion and pepper rings and serve.

PER SERVING:
    249 calories, 10g protein, 41g carbohydrates, 5g fat, 114mg sodium, 0mg cholesterol, 13g fiber

FRUITY VEGETABLE SALAD

The colorful combination of fruits and vegetables makes this a pretty salad and an elegant accompaniment to any meal.

PREPARATION TIME: 15 minutes NO COOKING SERVES: 4

FOR THE SALAD:

3 mandarin oranges, peeled and
    sectioned
½ fresh pineapple, cored, rind
    removed, and cut into chunks
1 cup seedless green or red grapes
1 green bell pepper, seeded and
    diced
1 red bell pepper, seeded and diced
1 cucumber, peeled and cut into
    thin rounds
1 carrot, peeled and cut into thin
    rounds

1 apple, cored and diced

FOR THE DRESSING:
1 cup plain yogurt cheese (p. 10)
2 Tbsp. chopped fresh cilantro
½ tsp. mustard powder
½ tsp. honey
¼ tsp. salt

GARNISH:
½ head cabbage, cut into bite-size
    chunks

1. In a bowl, combine the oranges, pineapple, grapes, bell peppers, cucumber, carrot, and apple. Chill.

2. In a separate bowl, whisk together the yogurt cheese, cilantro, mustard powder, honey, and salt. Chill for half an hour.

3. When you are ready to serve, transfer the salad ingredients to the center of a large platter. Arrange the cabbage around the rim of the platter. Drizzle the dressing over salad and cabbage. Serve.

PER SERVING:
    207 calories, 6g protein, 40g carbohydrates, 2.5g fat, 162mg sodium, 5mg
    cholesterol, 3g fiber

OKRA AND MIXED VEGETABLE SALAD

Okra is one of the most underrated vegetables. Always buy fresh, tender okra, and dry it thoroughly after washing. Salt it after cooking.

PREPARATION TIME: *15 minutes* COOKING TIME: *35 minutes* SERVES: 4

3 Tbsp. light vegetable oil
1 lb. okra, trimmed and cut into
 ¼-inch rounds
1 red onion, peeled and finely
 chopped
1 red bell pepper, seeded and finely
 chopped
1 green bell pepper, seeded and
 finely chopped

2 cups fresh corn kernels, cooked
 or 1 (10 oz.) can whole kernel
 corn, drained
1 tomato, diced
¼ tsp. paprika
¼ tsp. hot pepper sauce
¼ tsp. freshly ground black pepper
¼ tsp. salt or to taste

1. In a nonstick skillet, heat 2 tablespoons of the oil. Add the okra and let it sizzle undisturbed for a minute. Sauté the okra over medium-high heat for 20 minutes, stirring constantly, until tender but still crisp. Put it in a bowl and set aside.
2. In the same skillet, heat the remaining tablespoon of oil. Sauté the onion and bell peppers over medium heat until they are tender but still crisp. Add the corn, tomato, paprika, hot pepper sauce, black pepper, and salt, and sauté over medium heat for 5 minutes. Return the okra to the skillet and heat through for a minute. Serve.

PER SERVING:

145 calories, 3g protein, 22g carbohydrates, 5g fat, 357mg sodium, 0mg cholesterol, 1g fiber

TOMATO AND YOGURT SALAD (TOMATO RAITA)

This simple salad goes well with any spicy rice dish such as Rice Pilaf with Eggplant (p. 135). For best results, use beefsteak tomatoes.

PREPARATION TIME: *10 minutes* NO COOKING SERVES: 4

1 cup low-fat plain yogurt
½ cup low-fat sour cream
 (optional)
¼ tsp. salt

2 green chilies, minced
4 tomatoes, cored and cut into
 ½-inch dice
2 Tbsp. chopped fresh cilantro

In a bowl, combine the yogurt (and sour cream, if desired), salt, and green chilies. Just before serving, stir in the tomatoes and chopped cilantro.

PER SERVING:
> 102 calories, 5g protein, 10g carbohydrates, 4.5g fat, 159mg sodium, 10mg cholesterol, 1g fiber

SPINACH AND YOGURT SALAD (PALAK RAITA)

This soothing salad is quick and easy to make. You can substitute kale, collard greens, or any other greens of your choice for the spinach.

PREPARATION TIME: *5 minutes* COOKING TIME: *10 minutes* SERVES: 4

> *1 lb. fresh spinach, thoroughly cleaned (but not dried) and stemmed*
> *1 cup low-fat plain yogurt*
> *½ cup low-fat sour cream*
> *½ tsp. ground cumin*
>
> *½ tsp. ground coriander*
> *¼ tsp. freshly ground black pepper*
> *1 jalapeño pepper, finely minced*
> *¼ tsp. salt*
> *2 Tbsp. chopped fresh cilantro*

1. In a large saucepan, using only the water still on the leaves, steam the spinach for 5 to 10 minutes until limp. Drain and set aside.
2. In a bowl, combine the yogurt, sour cream, cumin, coriander, black pepper, jalapeño pepper, and salt. Fold the cooked spinach into the yogurt mixture. Sprinkle with cilantro and serve.

PER SERVING:
> 92 calories, 6g protein, 7.5g carbohydrates, 4g fat, 227mg sodium, 10mg cholesterol, 1g fiber

BANANA AND YOGURT SALAD (KELA RAITA)

*R*aisins impart a touch of sweetness to this salad. You can substitute seedless grapes, pineapple chunks, or peaches for the bananas.

PREPARATION TIME: *10 minutes* NO COOKING SERVES: 4

1 Tbsp. seedless golden raisins
½ cup hot water
1 cup low-fat plain yogurt
½ cup low-fat sour cream
1 Tbsp. honey

1 Tbsp. sugar
⅛ tsp. ground nutmeg
⅛ tsp. ground cardamom
2 firm, ripe bananas

1. Soak the raisins in the hot water to plump for 5 minutes. Drain.
2. In a bowl, combine the yogurt, sour cream, raisins, honey, sugar, nutmeg, and cardamom, and stir well. Refrigerate for 1 hour. Just before serving, peel and cut the banana into thick slices and fold into the yogurt mixture. Serve immediately.

PER SERVING:
   146 calories, 4g protein, 21g carbohydrates, 4.5g fat, 60mg sodium, 10mg cholesterol, 1g fiber

CUCUMBER AND YOGURT SALAD (KHEERA RAITA)

*P*eeled and chopped cucumbers are folded into seasoned yogurt for this refreshing salad. I prefer kirby cucumbers for this recipe, but feel free to substitute your favorite.

PREPARATION TIME: *15 minutes* NO COOKING SERVES: 4

4 *kirby cucumbers*
½ *tsp. salt*
1 *cup low-fat plain yogurt*

2 *tsp. fresh lime juice*
2 *Tbsp. chopped fresh cilantro*
¼ *tsp. cayenne pepper or paprika*

1. Peel and finely chop the cucumbers. Put them into a colander. Sprinkle with ¼ teaspoon of the salt and toss. Set aside. After 5 minutes, squeeze out the excess water from the cucumbers. Discard the water and reserve the cucumbers.
2. In a bowl, whisk the yogurt with a fork until smooth. Add the cucumbers, lime juice, chopped cilantro, and the remaining salt, and stir. To serve, sprinkle with cayenne pepper.

PER SERVING:
45 calories, 3g protein, 6g carbohydrates, 1g fat, 255mg sodium, 5mg cholesterol, 1g fiber

OKRA AND YOGURT SALAD (BHINDI RAITA)

*P*recooked okra is blended into yogurt just before serving.

PREPARATION TIME: *10 minutes* COOKING TIME: *20 minutes* SERVES: 4

2 *Tbsp. light vegetable oil*
1 *lb. okra, washed, dried, trimmed,*
   and cut into ¼-inch-thick rounds
1 *cup low-fat plain yogurt*

¼ *tsp. paprika or cayenne pepper*
½ *tsp. salt*
2 *Tbsp. chopped fresh cilantro*

1. In a large nonstick skillet, heat the oil. Add the okra and let it sizzle undisturbed for a minute. Sauté the okra over medium-high heat for about 15 minutes, until it is cooked through but still crispy. Remove the okra with a slotted spoon and drain on paper towels.
2. In a bowl, combine the yogurt, paprika, and salt. Just before serving, stir in the okra and garnish with chopped cilantro.

PER SERVING:

101 calories, 3.5g protein, 5g carbohydrates, 7g fat, 254mg sodium, 5mg cholesterol, 1.3g fiber

LIMA BEAN SALAD

*B*aby lima beans with bell pepper and onion make a simple and tasty salad.

PREPARATION TIME: *10 minutes* COOKING TIME: 20 *minutes* SERVES: 4

2 cups fresh lima beans, or 1 (20 oz.) package frozen lima beans
1 red onion, peeled and thinly sliced
1 red bell pepper, seeded and thinly sliced
½ cup scallions, thinly sliced

2 Tbsp. chopped fresh cilantro

FOR THE DRESSING:
1 cup yogurt cheese (p. 10)
¼ tsp. salt
½ tsp. freshly ground black pepper
¼ tsp. Tabasco sauce

1. In a saucepan with boiling water to cover, cook the lima beans for 8 to 10 minutes, until tender. Drain.
2. In a large salad bowl, mix the lima beans, onion, bell pepper, scallions, and cilantro.
3. In a separate bowl, combine the yogurt cheese, salt, black pepper, and Tabasco sauce. Mix well and drizzle over the salad. Serve warm or at room temperature.

PER SERVING:

162 calories, 10g protein, 26g carbohydrates, 2g fat, 254mg sodium, 5mg cholesterol, 4g fiber

RED KIDNEY BEAN, CHICKPEA, AND KOHLRABI SALAD

*K*ohlrabi is a pale green vegetable that resembles and tastes like a turnip. The kidney beans' bright red hue perks up this salad. I've included canned beans in this recipe, but if you have the time, don't hesitate to substitute dried beans that are pre-soaked and cooked (see instructions on page 159).

PREPARATION TIME: *15 minutes* NO COOKING SERVES: 4

1 (15 oz.) can red kidney beans, or
   1 cup dried red kidney beans,
   presoaked and cooked
1 (15 oz.) can chickpeas

FOR THE DRESSING:
1 Tbsp. extra-virgin olive oil
1 Tbsp. honey
2 Tbsp. fresh lime juice

⅛ tsp. hot sauce
2 Tbsp. finely chopped fresh
   cilantro

2 kohlrabi, peeled and cut into
   matchsticks
1 carrot, peeled and cut into
   matchsticks
1–2 green chilies or jalapeño
   peppers, seeded and minced

1. In a sieve, drain the kidney beans and chickpeas. Rinse thoroughly with water. Set aside.
2. In a jar with a tight-fitting lid, combine the dressing ingredients. Shake well.
3. In a large bowl, toss together the beans, chickpeas, kohlrabi, carrot, and green chilies. Dress the salad, and refrigerate. Serve chilled.

PER SERVING:
   165 calories, 9g protein, 26g carbohydrates, 2.5g fat, 124mg sodium, omg cholesterol, 12g fiber

CHICKPEA, CUCUMBER, AND BELL PEPPER SALAD

he oil-free yogurt dressing further enhances this snappy salad.

PREPARATION TIME: *20 minutes* NO COOKING SERVES: 4

FOR THE SALAD:
1 (15 oz.) can chickpeas
3 kirby cucumbers, peeled, cut in half lengthwise, and sliced thick
1 green bell pepper, seeded and chopped
1 red or yellow bell pepper, seeded and chopped
2 scallions, finely chopped

2 Tbsp. finely chopped fresh cilantro

FOR THE DRESSING:
½ cup low-fat plain yogurt
½ cup cottage cheese
¼ tsp. salt
¼ tsp. white pepper

1. In a sieve, drain the chickpeas; rinse under cold water and drain again. In a large bowl, combine the chickpeas, cucumbers, bell peppers, scallions, and cilantro. Chill.

2. In a small bowl, whisk together the yogurt, cottage cheese, salt, and white pepper. Just before serving, drizzle the dressing on the salad and toss.

PER SERVING:
134 calories, 10g protein, 19g carbohydrates, 2g fat, 248mg sodium, 2.5mg cholesterol, 7.5g fiber

CHAPTER 5

VEGETABLE CURRIES

....

CAULIFLOWER WITH TOMATOES

CAULIFLOWER AND GREEN PEA CURRY

CAULIFLOWER, POTATO, AND GREEN PEA CURRY

SAUTÉED EGGPLANT AND BELL PEPPER CURRY

SAUTÉED LIMA BEANS

SAUTÉED ASPARAGUS

POTATO, ONION, AND GREEN PEA CURRY

MUSHROOM AND ONION CURRY

MUSHROOM AND PEA CURRY

CORN AND GREEN BELL PEPPER CURRY

SAUTÉED BRUSSELS SPROUTS

SPICY GREEN BEANS

GREEN BEANS WITH ONION, GARLIC, AND TOMATO

GREEN BEANS IN YOGURT-ALMOND SAUCE

CHICKPEA CURRY

SPICY POTATO AND SWEET PEA CURRY

RED KIDNEY BEANS AND CABBAGE IN WHITE SAUCE

RED KIDNEY BEANS WITH VEGETABLES

SPICY GLAZED BEETS

BROCCOLI WITH GARLIC AND BLACK PEPPER

SPICY CABBAGE WITH PEAS AND TOMATOES

STIR-FRIED OKRA

OKRA STUFFED WITH SPICES IN YOGURT SAUCE

OKRA WITH TOMATOES AND GARLIC

STUFFED BELL PEPPERS IN TOMATO SAUCE

STUFFED MUSHROOMS

BAKED STUFFED TOMATOES

CORN-STUFFED POTATOES

STUFFED ZUCCHINI

WHOLE POTATOES IN SPICY YOGURT SAUCE

GREEN PEAS AND HOMEMADE CHEESE IN TOMATO SAUCE

SPINACH WITH HOMEMADE CHEESE

MIXED VEGETABLE KORMA

VEGETABLE STIR-FRY

MUSHROOMS AND BELL PEPPER CURRY

SPICED GREEN PLANTAINS

STUFFED EGGPLANT

ROASTED EGGPLANT IN TOMATO SAUCE

CHICKPEAS IN TOMATO, GINGER, AND GARLIC SAUCE

OVEN-ROASTED SPICED NEW POTATOES

VEGETABLE CURRIES

Explore the world of vegetables rich in nutritional values to prepare fabulous dishes that please the palate and satisfy the appetite. A little interest and touch of imagination can create an array of attractive and appealing gourmet dishes. The name "curry" is given to any dish that is prepared by cooking vegetables with a combination of spices—it need not have curry powder as an ingredient.

. . . .

CAULIFLOWER WITH TOMATOES

Tender cauliflowerets are simmered with tomatoes and mild spices. This dish goes well with Chapatis (p. 175) or Parathas (p. 178).

PREPARATION TIME: *15 minutes* COOKING TIME: *30 minutes* SERVES: 4

1 large cauliflower, cut into 1-inch florets
2 Tbsp. light vegetable oil
1 inch fresh ginger, peeled and minced
1–2 jalapeño peppers, stemmed and finely chopped (optional)

3 tomatoes, diced
½ tsp. ground coriander
½ tsp. ground cumin
½ tsp. cayenne pepper
½ tsp. salt

2 Tbsp. chopped fresh cilantro

1. In a saucepan with ¾ of an inch of water, place a steamer basket. Arrange the cauliflower evenly in the basket. Bring the water to a full boil over high heat, cover, and steam for 5 to 7 minutes, until the cauliflower is almost tender. Set aside.
2. In a large nonstick skillet or saucepan, heat the oil. Add the ginger (and jalapeño peppers, if desired) and sauté for 1 minute. Add the steamed cauliflower and tomatoes, and continue to sauté over medium heat for 10 minutes. Add the coriander, cumin, cayenne pepper, and salt; cook, stirring, for 2 minutes more. Garnish with the cilantro and serve hot.

PER SERVING:

112 calories, 3g protein, 9g carbohydrates, 7g fat, 227mg sodium, 0mg cholesterol, 2.8g fiber

CAULIFLOWER AND GREEN PEA CURRY

*I*f fresh peas aren't in season, you can prepare this dish with frozen peas for equally satisfying results. This dish goes well with Chapatis (p. 175).

PREPARATION TIME: *10 minutes* COOKING TIME: *25 minutes* SERVES: 4

1 head of cauliflower, cut into 1-inch florets
½ cup fresh or frozen peas
2 Tbsp. light vegetable oil
1 inch fresh ginger, peeled and minced
2 jalapeño peppers, stemmed and chopped
1 onion, peeled and chopped

2 ripe tomatoes, chopped
½ tsp. cayenne pepper
½ tsp. ground cumin
½ tsp. ground coriander
½ tsp. salt

½ cup low-fat plain yogurt
2 Tbsp. chopped fresh cilantro

1. In a saucepan, over ¼ of an inch of water, place a steamer basket. Arrange the cauliflower and peas in the basket. Bring the water to a full boil over high heat, cover, and steam for 5 to 7 minutes, until tender. Drain and set aside.
2. In a heavy nonstick large skillet or saucepan, heat the oil. Add the ginger, jalapeño peppers, and onion, and sauté for 3 to 4 minutes until the onion is golden. Stir in the cooked cauliflower and peas. Add the tomatoes, cayenne pepper, cumin, coriander, and salt, and cook, stirring, for 5 more minutes. Just before serving, add the yogurt and cilantro.

PER SERVING:

145 calories, 5g protein, 15g carbohydrates, 7g fat, 243mg sodium, 2.5mg cholesterol, 2.5g fiber

CAULIFLOWER, POTATO, AND GREEN PEA CURRY

This dish has a wonderfully thick consistency. You can serve it with Parathas (p. 178) or Pooris (p. 188).

PREPARATION TIME: *10 minutes* COOKING TIME: *25 minutes* SERVES: 4

1 small head of cauliflower, cut
into 1-inch florets
1 Tbsp. light vegetable oil
1 onion, peeled and thinly sliced
1 clove garlic, peeled and minced
2 potatoes, peeled and diced
1 cup fresh or thawed frozen peas
2 ripe tomatoes, diced
½ tsp. cayenne pepper

½ tsp. ground cumin
½ tsp. ground coriander
½ tsp. brown sugar
½ tsp. salt
1 cup water

¼ cup low-fat plain yogurt
2 Tbsp. chopped fresh cilantro

1. In a saucepan, over ¾ of an inch of water, place a steamer basket. Arrange the cauliflower in the basket. Bring the water to a full boil over high heat, cover, and steam for 5 to 7 minutes, until tender. Set cauliflower aside.

2. In a large nonstick skillet or saucepan, heat the oil. Add the onion and garlic, and sauté for 3 minutes. Add the potatoes and peas, and cook for 5 minutes over medium-low heat, until the potatoes are tender. Add the tomatoes, cayenne pepper, cumin, coriander, brown sugar, salt, the steamed cauliflower, and the water, and simmer over low heat for 5 minutes.

3. Just before serving, remove the skillet from the heat and add the yogurt and cilantro.

PER SERVING:
144 calories, 5g protein, 22g carbohydrates, 4g fat, 222mg sodium, 1mg cholesterol, 3g fiber

SAUTÉED EGGPLANT AND BELL PEPPER CURRY

A touch of garam masala accents the natural flavors of the eggplant and bell peppers.

PREPARATION TIME: *10 minutes* COOKING TIME: *20 minutes* SERVES: 4

2 Tbsp. light vegetable oil
1 onion, peeled, halved, and thinly sliced
3 green bell peppers, seeded and cut into ½-inch cubes
1 large eggplant or 4 small Italian eggplants, cut into ½-inch cubes

½ tsp. garam masala (p. 25)
½ tsp. cayenne pepper
¼ tsp. salt
¼ cup low-fat plain yogurt

2 Tbsp. chopped fresh cilantro

In a large nonstick saucepan or skillet, heat the oil. Add the onion and sauté until golden. Stir in the bell peppers and eggplant; sauté for 5 to 7 minutes, until the vegetables are tender but still firm to the bite. Add the garam masala, cayenne pepper, and salt, and simmer over low heat for 2 to 3 minutes. Add the yogurt and mix well. Remove from the heat, garnish with the cilantro, and serve.

PER SERVING:
112 calories, 3g protein, 9g carbohydrates, 7g fat, 113mg sodium, 1mg cholesterol, 1.5g fiber

SAUTÉED LIMA BEANS

*L*ima beans have a creamy texture and a sweet, meaty flavor. Making this dish with frozen lima beans turns it into a year-round favorite.

PREPARATION TIME: *10 minutes* COOKING TIME: *20 minutes* SERVES: *4*

1 Tbsp. light vegetable or olive oil
1 red onion, peeled, halved, and
    thinly sliced
2 cloves garlic, peeled and minced
2 jalapeño peppers, stemmed and
    finely sliced
1 (10 oz.) package thawed frozen
    lima beans

2 tsp. fresh lime juice
¼ tsp. cayenne pepper
¼ tsp. salt
1 Tbsp. fresh bread crumbs

2 Tbsp. chopped fresh cilantro or
    parsley

1. In a large nonstick skillet or saucepan, heat the oil. Add the onion, garlic, and jalapeño peppers, and sauté for 2 to 3 minutes. Stir in the lima beans and cook for 10 minutes more, until the beans are tender. Add the lime juice, cayenne pepper, salt, and bread crumbs; sauté for 2 minutes.
2. Garnish with the chopped cilantro. This dish can be served either hot or at room temperature.

PER SERVING:
    144 calories, 6g protein, 21g carbohydrates, 4g fat, 256mg sodium, 0mg
    cholesterol, 5g fiber

SAUTÉED ASPARAGUS

*T*ender asparagus sautéed in olive oil and seasoned with garlic. If you prefer, you can substitute broccoli florets for asparagus for equally satisfying results.

PREPARATION TIME: *10 minutes* COOKING TIME: *15 minutes* SERVES: 4

2 Tbsp. olive oil
2 cloves garlic, peeled and minced
3 lbs. asparagus, cleaned, trimmed,
    and cut into 1-inch pieces

2 Tbsp. water
¼ tsp. cayenne pepper
¼ tsp. salt

1. In a large nonstick skillet, heat the oil. Add the garlic and sauté over medium-low heat until it turns golden, taking care not to burn it. Add the asparagus and water, and sauté for 5 to 7 minutes over medium-high heat, until the asparagus is tender but still firm.
2. Add the cayenne pepper and salt, and stir gently. Serve hot.

PER SERVING:

124 calories, 5g protein, 10g carbohydrates, 7g fat, 111mg sodium, 0mg cholesterol, 2g fiber

POTATO, ONION, AND GREEN PEA CURRY

This creamy curry has a unique flavor and texture. It goes well with Chapatis (p. 175) or pita bread.

PREPARATION TIME: *15 minutes* COOKING TIME: *25 minutes* SERVES: 4

2 Tbsp. light vegetable oil	¼ tsp. ground coriander
2 onions, peeled and cubed	½ tsp. curry powder
2 potatoes, peeled and cubed	¼ tsp. salt
½ cup fresh or thawed frozen peas	¼ tsp. brown sugar
2 ripe tomatoes, diced	
¼ tsp. cayenne pepper	3 Tbsp. low-fat plain yogurt
¼ tsp. ground cumin	2 Tbsp. chopped fresh cilantro

1. In a large nonstick saucepan, heat the oil. Add the onions and sauté until they turn golden. Add the potatoes and peas, and sauté over medium heat for 5 to 7 minutes, until the potatoes are tender. Stir in the tomatoes, cayenne pepper, cumin, coriander, curry powder, salt, and brown sugar, and simmer for 5 minutes more.
2. Just before serving, add the yogurt and garnish with the cilantro. Serve hot or warm.

PER SERVING:

154 calories, 3g protein, 17g carbohydrates, 8g fat, 112mg sodium, 1mg cholesterol, 3g fiber

MUSHROOM AND ONION CURRY

*F*resh mushrooms sautéed with onions and laced with spices make this a delectable dish. This dish goes well with any Indian bread (see Chapter 8).

PREPARATION TIME: *10 minutes* COOKING TIME: *20 minutes* SERVES: 4

2 Tbsp. light vegetable oil	1 tomato, diced
2 onions, peeled and coarsely chopped	⅛ tsp. cayenne pepper
	½ tsp. curry powder
1¼ lbs. cultivated or button mushrooms, halved	½ tsp. ground cumin
	¼ tsp. salt or to taste

In a large nonstick skillet, heat the oil and add the onions. Sauté until golden. Add the mushrooms and tomato, and simmer over medium heat for 8 to 10 minutes, stirring occasionally. Add the cayenne pepper, curry powder, cumin, and salt; stir well. Cook for 2 more minutes and serve hot.

PER SERVING:
124 calories, 3g protein, 10g carbohydrates, 8g fat, 110mg sodium, 0mg cholesterol, 2g fiber

MUSHROOM AND PEA CURRY

*T*his multicolored dish has great eye appeal, especially when served with plain white rice or Indian bread.

PREPARATION TIME: *10 minutes* COOKING TIME: *25 minutes* SERVES: 4

2 Tbsp. vegetable oil

2 cloves garlic, peeled and minced

1 inch fresh ginger, peeled and grated

1¼ lbs. cultivated or button mushrooms, halved lengthwise

1 cup fresh or thawed frozen peas

¼ cup water

1 ripe tomato, diced

½ tsp. ground cumin

½ tsp. ground coriander

½ tsp. cayenne pepper

¼ tsp. garam masala (p. 25)

½ tsp. salt or to taste

In a 3-quart nonstick saucepan, heat the oil. Add the garlic and ginger, and sauté for 1 minute. Add the mushrooms, peas, and water, and bring to a simmer. Cover and cook over medium-low heat for 10 minutes, until the vegetables are tender. Stir in the tomato, cumin, coriander, cayenne pepper, garam masala, and salt. Simmer for 5 minutes more to blend the flavors. Serve hot or warm.

PER SERVING:

143 calories, 6g protein, 14g carbohydrates, 7g fat, 222mg sodium, 0mg cholesterol, 2g fiber

CORN AND GREEN BELL PEPPER CURRY

The natural sweetness of corn mellows the flavor of this spicy curry.

PREPARATION TIME: *10 minutes*   COOKING TIME: *20 minutes*   SERVES: 4

2 Tbsp. light vegetable oil

2 red onions, peeled, halved, and thinly sliced

1–2 jalapeño peppers, stemmed and thinly sliced

2 green bell peppers, seeded and diced

1 cup fresh corn kernels, or 1 (10 oz.) package thawed frozen corn, or 1 (17 oz.) can whole kernel corn, drained and rinsed

½ tsp. curry powder

⅛ tsp. cayenne pepper

1 Tbsp. fresh lime juice

¼ tsp. salt or to taste

1 ripe tomato, thinly sliced

In a large nonstick skillet, heat the oil. Add the onions and jalapeño peppers, and sauté for 3 minutes. Add the bell peppers and corn, and sauté, stirring, over medium heat until all the vegetables are tender but still crisp. Add the curry powder, cayenne pepper, lime juice, and salt, and simmer over low heat for 2 minutes more. Serve hot, garnished with tomato slices.

PER SERVING:
    135 calories, 3g protein, 15g carbohydrates, 7g fat, 112mg sodium, omg cholesterol, 2g fiber

SAUTÉED BRUSSELS SPROUTS

A variety of spices pep up this fiber-rich vegetable. This simple dish goes well with Chapatis (p. 175).

PREPARATION TIME: *10 minutes* COOKING TIME: *15 minutes* SERVES: 4

2 Tbsp. light vegetable oil	½ tsp. ground cumin
3 onions, peeled and diced	½ tsp. ground coriander
2 jalapeño peppers, stemmed and	½ tsp. cayenne pepper
finely chopped	¼ tsp. salt
1 lb. fresh Brussels sprouts,	
cleaned, trimmed, and halved	

In a 3-quart nonstick saucepan, heat the oil. Add the onions and jalapeño peppers, and sauté for 3 minutes. Add the Brussels sprouts and sauté over medium-low heat for 10 minutes, until the sprouts are tender when pierced with a fork. Stir in the cumin, coriander, cayenne pepper, and salt, and simmer for 2 to 3 minutes more. Serve hot or warm.

PER SERVING:
    120 calories, 3g protein, 11g carbohydrates, 7g fat, 115mg sodium, omg cholesterol, 5g fiber

SPICY GREEN BEANS

*L*ook for fresh, bright green beans for maximum flavor.

PREPARATION TIME: *10 minutes* COOKING TIME: *20 minutes* SERVES: 4

*1 lb. fresh green beans, trimmed
and cut into 1-inch pieces
1 Tbsp. vegetable or olive oil
½ tsp. cumin seeds
2 cloves garlic, peeled and minced*

*1–2 green chilies or jalapeño
peppers, stemmed and finely
chopped, or ¼ tsp. crushed red
pepper
½ tsp. salt*

*1 Tbsp. finely chopped fresh
cilantro*

1. In a saucepan in enough water to cover, boil the beans for about 15 minutes, until they are tender. Drain and set aside.
2. In a large nonstick skillet, heat the oil. Add the cumin seeds, garlic, and green chilies, and sauté for 2 minutes, until the garlic is a pale gold. Add the beans and salt, and cook at a low simmer for about 2 minutes. Garnish with the cilantro and serve hot.

PER SERVING:
    70 calories, 2g protein, 8g carbohydrates, 3.5g fat, 215mg sodium, 0mg cholesterol, 2g fiber

GREEN BEANS WITH ONION, GARLIC, AND TOMATO

*S*auté crisp cooked beans with tomatoes and garlic for a zippier taste.

PREPARATION TIME: *10 minutes* COOKING TIME: *20 minutes* SERVES: 4

1 lb. green beans, trimmed and cut
into ½-inch pieces
1 Tbsp. extra-virgin olive oil
2 red onions, halved and thinly
sliced

2 cloves garlic, peeled and minced
2 ripe tomatoes, diced
½ tsp. cayenne pepper
¼ tsp. salt or to taste

1. In a saucepan in enough water to cover, boil the beans over medium heat for 12
to 15 minutes, until the beans are tender but still crisp. Drain and set aside.

2. In a large nonstick skillet, heat the oil. Add the onions and garlic, and sauté over
medium heat for 4 to 5 minutes, until the onions are soft and translucent. Add the
tomatoes, beans, cayenne pepper, and salt, and simmer for 5 minutes until the flavors are blended. Serve hot with buttered rice.

PER SERVING:

98 calories, 3g protein, 12g carbohydrates, 4g fat, 112mg sodium, 0mg
cholesterol, 3g fiber

GREEN BEANS IN YOGURT-ALMOND SAUCE

The yogurt and almond sauce adds a slightly piquant yet sweet flavor and
extra texture to this dish.

PREPARATION TIME: 10 minutes COOKING TIME: 20 minutes SERVES: 4

1 lb. green beans, trimmed and cut
into 1-inch pieces
1 Tbsp. extra-virgin olive oil
2 jalapeño peppers, stemmed and
minced
2 cloves garlic, peeled and minced
1 inch fresh ginger, peeled and
minced
½ tsp. ground cumin

½ tsp. ground coriander
½ tsp. ground nutmeg
2 Tbsp. coarsely powdered
almonds, or 1 Tbsp. almond
paste
½ tsp. salt or to taste
½ cup low-fat plain yogurt

2 Tbsp. chopped fresh cilantro

1. In a saucepan in enough water to cover, boil the beans over medium heat for 12 to 15 minutes, until they are tender but still crisp. Drain and set aside.
2. In a large nonstick skillet or saucepan, heat the oil. Add the jalapeño peppers, garlic, and ginger, and sauté for 2 to 3 minutes, until the garlic is soft. Stir in the beans, cumin, coriander, nutmeg, ground almonds, salt, and yogurt. Sauté, stirring, over low heat, until the sauce thickens. Garnish with the cilantro and serve hot or warm.

PER SERVING:
  122 calories, 5g protein, 12g carbohydrates, 6g fat, 236mg sodium, 2.5mg cholesterol, 3g fiber

CHICKPEA CURRY

Chickpeas, rich in minerals and vitamins, are one of the best-tasting legumes. Canned chickpeas, which I have used for this recipe, are an acceptable substitute for dried chickpeas. If you do use dried beans, however, see cooking instructions on page 159.

PREPARATION TIME: *10 minutes* COOKING TIME: *20 minutes* SERVES: 4

2 Tbsp. vegetable oil
2 onions, peeled, halved, and thinly sliced
1 (20 oz.) can chickpeas, drained and rinsed, or 1¼ cup dried chickpeas, presoaked and cooked
2 potatoes, peeled, cubed, and boiled
½ tsp. cayenne pepper
½ tsp. garam masala (p. 25)
½ tsp. ground coriander

¼ tsp. ground cumin
1 Tbsp. fresh lime juice
½ tsp. salt or to taste
¼ cup water

FOR GARNISH:
¼ cup low-fat plain yogurt
1 tomato, thinly sliced
2 Tbsp. chopped fresh cilantro

1. In a large nonstick skillet, heat the oil. Add the onions and sauté for 5 minutes, until the onions are soft. Add the chickpeas, cooked potatoes, cayenne pepper, garam masala, coriander, cumin, lime juice, salt, and water, and simmer for 5 minutes.

2. Serve in individual bowls garnished with 1 tablespoon of yogurt, a slice of tomato, and chopped cilantro.

PER SERVING:
 256 calories, 10g protein, 36g carbohydrates, 8g fat, 230mg sodium, 1.2mg cholesterol, 8g fiber

SPICY POTATO AND SWEET PEA CURRY

*P*otatoes and peas are cooked in spices and seasoned in yogurt. This hearty dish goes well with Chapatis (p. 175) or Pooris (p. 188).

PREPARATION TIME: *10 minutes* COOKING TIME: *25 minutes* SERVES: 4

2 Tbsp. vegetable oil	½–1 tsp. chili powder
1 onion, peeled, halved, and thinly sliced	½ tsp. garam masala (p. 25)
	½ tsp. ground cumin
1 inch fresh ginger, peeled and grated	½ tsp. ground coriander
	1 Tbsp. fresh lime juice
½ tsp. ground turmeric	½ tsp. salt or to taste
2 ripe tomatoes, chopped	5 potatoes, peeled, boiled, and cut into 1-inch chunks
1 (10 oz.) package frozen tiny sweet peas, cooked according to package directions	½ cup low-fat plain yogurt
	2 Tbsp. chopped fresh cilantro

1. In a large nonstick saucepan, heat the oil. Add the onion, ginger, and turmeric, and sauté for 5 minutes, until the onion is soft. Add the tomatoes, peas, chili powder, garam masala, cumin, coriander, lime juice, and salt, and simmer over medium-low heat for 5 minutes.

2. Add the cooked potatoes and yogurt, and heat gently over low heat. Be careful not to boil the mixture or the yogurt will separate. Garnish with the chopped cilantro and serve hot.

PER SERVING:
256 calories, 8g protein, 36g carbohydrates, 8g fat, 290mg sodium, 2.5mg cholesterol, 5g fiber

RED KIDNEY BEANS AND CABBAGE IN WHITE SAUCE

I have experimented with several types of cheeses for this recipe, and my preference is mozzarella.

PREPARATION TIME: *10 minutes* COOKING TIME: *25 minutes* SERVES: 4

*2 potatoes, peeled and cut into
  ¼-inch-thick rounds
1 Tbsp. olive oil
1 onion, peeled and finely chopped
1 (17 oz.) can red kidney beans,
  drained and rinsed
3 Tbsp. tomato sauce
½ tsp. cayenne pepper*

*½ tsp. curry powder
Salt and black pepper to taste
1 small head cabbage, broken into
  leaves and blanched in salted
  boiling water
1 cup white sauce (p. 28)
4 Tbsp. part-skim mozzarella
  cheese, shredded (optional)*

1. Preheat oven to 350 degrees.
2. Salt and pepper the potatoes. Set aside.
3. In a nonstick skillet, heat the oil. Add the onion and sauté until it turns golden. Add the beans, tomato sauce, cayenne pepper, curry powder, and salt, and simmer for 5 minutes.
4. Oil a baking dish with vegetable cooking spray. Arrange the blanched cabbage leaves on the bottom. Pour the bean mixture over the leaves and top with the potato rounds. Pour the white sauce over the potatoes and sprinkle evenly with the shredded cheese. Bake for 20 minutes. Serve hot.

PER SERVING:
> 210 calories, 7g protein, 31g carbohydrates, 6g fat, 250mg sodium, 4mg cholesterol, 8g fiber

RED KIDNEY BEANS WITH VEGETABLES

This simple, snappy dish is a nutritional bonanza.

PREPARATION TIME: *10 minutes* COOKING TIME: *30 minutes* SERVES: 4

2 Tbsp. olive oil
3 onions, peeled, halved, and thinly sliced
2 cloves garlic, peeled and minced
2 carrots, peeled, halved, and thinly sliced
2 green bell peppers, seeded and thinly sliced

1 (16 oz.) can red kidney beans, drained and rinsed
½ tsp. cayenne pepper
1 Tbsp. fresh lime juice
½ cup spicy tomato sauce (p. 27)
2 ripe tomatoes, chopped
½–¾ tsp. salt

In a large nonstick skillet or saucepan, heat the oil. Add the onions and garlic, and sauté for 2 minutes. Add the carrots and bell peppers, and sauté for 5 minutes more, until the vegetables are tender. Add the beans, cayenne pepper, lime juice, tomato sauce, tomatoes, and salt. Sauté over medium-low heat for 5 minutes. Serve hot.

PER SERVING:
> 220 calories, 9g protein, 30g carbohydrates, 7g fat, 200mg sodium, 0mg cholesterol, 8g fiber

SPICY GLAZED BEETS

*T*his tangy, sweet dish is colorful and can be served as a side dish or as a topping for a crunchy salad.

PREPARATION TIME: *15 minutes* COOKING TIME: *20 minutes* SERVES: 4

4 *fresh beets (approximately 1 lb.)*	½ *tsp. cayenne pepper*
2 *Tbsp. vegetable oil*	½ *tsp. salt*
1 *onion, peeled, halved, and thinly sliced*	
1–2 *jalapeño peppers, stemmed and minced*	2 *Tbsp. grated fresh coconut or dried coconut powder, if available*

1. With a vegetable peeler, peel the beets and cut into ¼-inch sticks.
2. In a saucepan in enough water to cover, boil the beets for 10 to 12 minutes, until tender. Drain and rinse the beets until they stop shedding their color or until the water runs clear.
3. In a nonstick skillet, heat the oil. Add the onion and jalapeño peppers, and sauté until the onion is soft. Add the cooked beets, cayenne pepper, and salt, and cook for 2 minutes more, stirring occasionally. Sprinkle the coconut on top and serve hot, warm, or cold.

PER SERVING:
114 calories, 2g protein, 10g carbohydrates, 7g fat, 215mg sodium, 0mg cholesterol, 3g fiber

BROCCOLI WITH GARLIC AND BLACK PEPPER

*P*erk up this fiber-rich vegetable with garlic and pepper for a nutritious side dish.

PREPARATION TIME: *10 minutes* COOKING TIME: *20 minutes* SERVES: 4

1 Tbsp. virgin olive oil
5 cloves garlic, peeled and thinly sliced
1 large head of broccoli, trimmed, chopped, and cooked according to your favorite method, or 2 (10 oz.) packages frozen chopped broccoli, cooked according to package directions

½ tsp. salt
1 tsp. freshly ground black pepper
2 Tbsp. powdered dry coconut or finely ground cashews

In a nonstick skillet over low heat, heat the oil. Add the garlic and sauté until it turns golden. Be careful not to burn the garlic. Add the broccoli, salt, pepper, and coconut or cashews. Sauté for 2 minutes, until all the ingredients are well incorporated. Serve with buttered rice.

PER SERVING:
118 calories, 5g protein, 8g carbohydrates, 7g fat, 215mg sodium, omg cholesterol, 3g fiber

SPICY CABBAGE WITH PEAS AND TOMATOES

Cabbage is sautéed and simmered to release its sweet flavor. This dish can be prepared in advance, refrigerated, and reheated. Serve with any Indian bread or plain rice.

PREPARATION TIME: *15 minutes* COOKING TIME: *20 minutes* SERVES: 4

2 Tbsp. vegetable oil
2 onions, peeled and thinly sliced
1 inch fresh ginger, peeled and
    chopped
1 head of cabbage, shredded
1 cup fresh peas, or 1 (10 oz.)
    package thawed frozen sweet
    tender peas

2 ripe tomatoes, diced
¼–½ tsp. cayenne pepper
½ tsp. ground coriander
½ tsp. ground cumin
½ tsp. salt

In a large nonstick skillet, heat the oil. Add the onions and sauté until soft. Stir in the ginger, cabbage, peas, and tomatoes, and simmer, covered, over low heat for 10 to 12 minutes, until the cabbage is limp. Add the cayenne pepper, coriander, cumin, and salt, and simmer for 5 minutes more. Serve with plain rice.

PER SERVING:
    168 calories, 6g protein, 20g carbohydrates, 7g fat, 270mg sodium, 0mg cholesterol, 7g fiber

STIR-FRIED OKRA

Except in the South, okra is an underappreciated vegetable in this country. If properly cooked, okra is delicious. Just remember to wipe the okra thoroughly dry after washing and add salt after it is fully cooked.

PREPARATION TIME: 15 minutes COOKING TIME: 25 minutes SERVES: 4

    1 lb. fresh okra
    2 Tbsp. vegetable oil
    ½ tsp. cayenne pepper
    ½ tsp. salt

1. Wash the okra and wipe it completely dry with paper towels to prevent stickiness. Trim both ends and slice the okra into ¼-inch-thick rounds.

2. In a large nonstick skillet, heat the oil. Add the okra, let it sizzle undisturbed for 1 minute, and cook over medium-high heat for 20 minutes, stirring constantly, until the okra is cooked through but still firm. Remove from the heat, then stir in the cayenne pepper and salt.

PER SERVING:
   84 calories, 2g protein, 3g carbohydrates, 6.5g fat, 210mg sodium, omg cholesterol, 1g fiber

OKRA STUFFED WITH SPICES IN YOGURT SAUCE

Okra is slit and stuffed with spices. Its flavor is further enhanced by the yogurt sauce.

PREPARATION TIME: *15 minutes* COOKING TIME: *25 minutes* SERVES: 4

1 lb. fresh okra	*2 onions, peeled and chopped*
½–1 tsp. cayenne pepper or paprika	*1 ripe tomato, chopped*
1 tsp. ground cumin	*¼ cup water*
1 tsp. ground coriander	*½ tsp. salt*
1½ tsp. vegetable oil	*¼ cup thick, plain yogurt*

1. Wash the okra and wipe it completely dry with paper towels. Cut off the stem, and with a sharp pointed knife, make a slit along the length of each okra.
2. In a small bowl, mix the cayenne pepper, cumin, and coriander. Holding the okra slit open in one hand, spread a little spice mixture in the slit with a butter knife. Repeat the process until all the okra pods are stuffed. Set aside.
3. In a nonstick skillet, heat the oil. Add the onions and sauté for about 5 minutes until golden. Add the stuffed okra and sauté for about 5 minutes. Add the tomato and water, and simmer, covered, over medium heat for 10 to 15 minutes, until the okra is tender. Stir in the salt and any leftover spice mixture, and remove from the heat.
4. Beat the yogurt with a wire whisk to a creamy texture. Combine with the okra just before serving.

PER SERVING:
    87 calories, 3g protein, 7g carbohydrates, 5g fat, 227mg sodium, 1mg
    cholesterol, 1g fiber

OKRA WITH TOMATOES AND GARLIC

*B*lack pepper lends a special flavor to this okra dish.

PREPARATION TIME: *10 minutes* COOKING TIME: *20 minutes* SERVES: 4

1 lb. fresh okra
2 Tbsp. virgin olive oil
2 onions, peeled and chopped
3 cloves garlic, peeled and minced

2 ripe tomatoes, chopped
⅛ tsp. freshly ground black pepper
2 Tbsp. water
½ tsp. salt

1. Wash the okra and wipe it completely dry with paper towels. Trim both ends and cut the okra into ¼-inch-thick rounds.
2. In a large nonstick skillet, heat the oil. Add the onions and garlic, and sauté over medium heat until the onions just begin to soften. Add the okra and continue sautéing for 2 minutes. Stir in the tomatoes, pepper, and water, and simmer gently over low heat for 20 minutes, until the okra is tender. Add the salt and serve hot or at room temperature.

PER SERVING:
    105 calories, 2g protein, 8g carbohydrates, 7g fat, 220mg sodium, 0mg
    cholesterol, 1.5g fiber

STUFFED BELL PEPPERS IN TOMATO SAUCE

*Y*ou may use frozen mixed vegetables for convenience in this recipe, but I encourage you to substitute fresh vegetables in season.

PREPARATION TIME: *20 minutes* COOKING TIME: *30 minutes* SERVES: 4

8 green or red bell peppers

FOR THE STUFFING:
1 Tbsp. vegetable oil
1 (16 oz.) package of thawed
   frozen mixed vegetables
   (broccoli, cauliflower, peas,
   anything you like)
¼ tsp. cayenne pepper
½ tsp. ground cumin
¼ tsp. salt or to taste

2 potatoes, peeled, boiled, and
   mashed

FOR THE TOMATO SAUCE:
1 (15 oz.) can tomato puree
½ tsp. cayenne pepper or paprika
½ tsp. ground cumin
½ tsp. ground cinnamon
2 tsp. brown sugar or honey
¼ tsp. salt or to taste
2 Tbsp. grated Parmesan cheese

1. Preheat the oven to 350 degrees.
2. Cut the tops off the peppers and scoop out the seeds. Drop them in boiling water to cover for 3 minutes. Drain and set aside.
3. To prepare the stuffing:
In a nonstick sauté pan, heat the oil. Cook the thawed vegetables for 8 to 10 minutes, until they are tender but still firm. Add the cayenne pepper, cumin, salt, and mashed potatoes; stir to combine. Set aside.
4. To prepare the tomato sauce:
In a saucepan, combine the tomato puree, cayenne pepper, cumin, cinnamon, brown sugar, and salt. Boil, stirring, for 10 minutes, until the sauce thickens.
5. Fill the bell peppers with an equal amount of stuffing, and place them cut side up in a baking pan brushed with oil. Pour the hot tomato sauce over the peppers and sprinkle with the grated cheese. Bake for 10 minutes. Serve hot.

PER SERVING:
   179 calories, 8g protein, 25g carbohydrates, 5g fat, 170mg sodium, 2mg cholesterol, 3.5g fiber

STUFFED MUSHROOMS

Select large, firm mushrooms for this low-fat, high-protein dish because they have a stronger flavor and are easier to stuff.

PREPARATION TIME: *10 minutes* COOKING TIME: *15 minutes* SERVES: 4

1 Tbsp. virgin olive oil
1 onion, peeled and finely chopped
1 green bell pepper, seeded and
  finely chopped
1 cup fresh bread crumbs
¼ tsp. cayenne pepper
¼ tsp. salt

1 tsp. fresh lime juice
2 Tbsp. finely chopped fresh
  cilantro or parsley
2 Tbsp. grated Parmesan cheese
  (optional)
20 fresh large mushrooms,
  stemmed and cleaned

1. Preheat the oven to 350 degrees.
2. In a nonstick saucepan, heat the oil. Add the onion and bell pepper, and sauté, stirring, for 2 minutes. Stir in the bread crumbs, cayenne pepper, salt, lime juice, and cilantro. Simmer for 2 minutes.
3. Fill the mushroom caps with the stuffing (sprinkle with grated Parmesan cheese, if desired). In a casserole large enough to fit them in one layer, bake for 10 to 15 minutes, or run them under a preheated broiler for 10 minutes. Serve hot.

PER SERVING:
  103 calories, 5g protein, 11g carbohydrates, 4g fat, 147mg sodium, 2mg cholesterol, 1g fiber

BAKED STUFFED TOMATOES

*T*omato shells are stuffed with spiced rice and baked until tender.

PREPARATION TIME: *20 minutes* COOKING TIME: *25 minutes* SERVES: 4

8 ripe tomatoes
1 Tbsp. olive oil
1 onion, peeled and chopped
1–2 jalapeño peppers, stemmed,
  seeded, and minced, to taste
1 cup fresh or frozen peas, cooked
  according to preferred method

1 cup long-grain rice, cooked
Salt to taste
2 Tbsp. chopped fresh cilantro
2 Tbsp. grated Parmesan cheese

1. Preheat the oven to 350 degrees.

2. Cut the tops off the tomatoes and reserve. With a spoon, carefully remove the pulp from each tomato and reserve.

3. In a nonstick saucepan, heat the oil. Add the onion and jalapeño peppers and sauté over medium heat for 5 minutes, until the onion is wilted. Add the peas and rice, and cook over medium-low heat for 2 to 3 minutes. Add the tomato pulp, salt, and cilantro, and simmer for 2 minutes more. Fill the tomatoes with the rice mixture, and sprinkle the cheese on top. Bake in a gratin dish for 15 minutes.

4. Replace the tops on the tomatoes and serve hot.

PER SERVING:
249 calories, 8g protein, 43g carbohydrates, 5g fat, 250mg sodium, 2mg cholesterol, 5g fiber

CORN-STUFFED POTATOES

*T*ender, sweet corn is laced with salt and pepper and stuffed into baked potatoes.

PREPARATION TIME: *10 minutes* COOKING TIME: *40 minutes* SERVES: 4

4 large baking potatoes	1 (17 oz.) can sweet whole kernel
2 Tbsp. vegetable oil	corn, or 2 cups fresh corn kernels
1 onion, peeled and finely chopped	1 ripe tomato, chopped
2 jalapeño peppers, stemmed,	½ tsp. freshly ground black pepper
seeded, and chopped	¼ tsp. salt or to taste

1. Preheat the oven to 350 degrees.

2. Brush the potatoes with oil, wrap them in aluminum foil, and bake them for 25 to 30 minutes. Cool and cut in half horizontally. Scoop out the insides and mash, reserving the skin intact. Set aside the mashed potatoes.

3. In a sauté pan, heat the oil. Add the onion and jalapeño peppers. Sauté, stirring, for 2 minutes. Add the corn, chopped tomato, mashed potatoes, black pepper, and salt, and simmer for 3 to 4 minutes.

4. Fill the potato skins with the corn stuffing and bake in a gratin dish for 6 minutes. Serve hot.

PER SERVING:

194 calories, 4g protein, 28g carbohydrates, 7g fat, 117mg sodium, omg cholesterol, 6.2g fiber

STUFFED ZUCCHINI

Flavorful zucchini shells are stuffed with rice and tomatoes and baked until tender. If you prefer you can substitute a combination of vegetables for the rice.

PREPARATION TIME: *10 minutes* COOKING TIME: *35 minutes* SERVES: 4

4 medium zucchini	*2 Tbsp. fresh bread crumbs*
1 Tbsp. olive oil	*¼ tsp. chili powder*
1 onion, peeled and chopped	*1 Tbsp. fresh lime or lemon juice*
1 clove garlic, peeled and minced	*¼ tsp. salt or to taste*
2 ripe tomatoes, diced	*1 cup spicy tomato sauce (p. 27)*
1 cup white or brown rice, cooked	*(can be canned)*

1. Preheat the oven to 350 degrees.
2. Cut each zucchini in half lengthwise. With a sharp knife or melon baller, scoop out the insides, leaving a ¼-inch shell. Finely chop the flesh and reserve.
3. In a nonstick skillet, heat the oil. Add the onion and garlic, and sauté for 5 minutes over medium heat, until the onion is soft. Add the chopped zucchini flesh and tomatoes, and sauté for 2 to 3 minutes. Stir in the cooked rice, bread crumbs, chili powder, lime juice, and salt. Simmer for 2 minutes, until the flavors are well blended.
4. Fill each zucchini shell with an equal portion of the stuffing. Cover and bake in a casserole dish for 30 to 40 minutes. Serve hot with spicy tomato sauce (p. 27).

PER SERVING:

208 calories, 5g protein, 38g carbohydrates, 4g fat, 112mg sodium, omg cholesterol, 2g fiber

WHOLE POTATOES IN SPICY YOGURT SAUCE
(DUM ALOO)

*T*ry one of India's most popular dishes. Potatoes are a wonderful medium for these zesty flavorings.

PREPARATION TIME: *15 minutes* COOKING TIME: *1 hour, 30 minutes* SERVES: 4

12 small new red potatoes or baby white potatoes, peeled
2 Tbsp. vegetable oil
2 onions, peeled and chopped
2 cloves garlic, peeled and chopped
1 inch fresh ginger, peeled and chopped
½ tsp. ground turmeric
2 tsp. ground coriander

1 tsp. ground cumin
½ tsp. garam masala (p. 25)
¼ tsp. ground cardamom
¼ tsp. chili powder
¼ tsp. salt or to taste
¼ cup finely ground cashews
2 ripe tomatoes, chopped, or 1 cup canned tomato sauce
1 cup low-fat plain yogurt

1. Preheat the oven to 350 degrees.

2. Prick the potatoes with a sharp knife in two or three places. Arrange them on a baking dish and spray with vegetable oil cooking spray. Bake for 45 to 50 minutes until they begin to brown and become crisp. Set aside.

3. In a 4-quart nonstick saucepan, heat the oil. Add the onions and sauté over medium-high heat for 5 minutes, until they turn golden. Add the garlic, ginger, and turmeric, and sauté for 2 minutes. Stir in the coriander, cumin, garam masala, cardamom, chili powder, salt, ground cashews, and chopped tomatoes. Sauté for 5 minutes. Beat the yogurt with a wire whisk until it is smooth and creamy, and add it to the saucepan. Stir in the baked potatoes and simmer gently, covered, over low heat for 30 minutes, until the sauce is thick enough to coat the potatoes, stirring occasionally to make sure the mixture is not sticking to the bottom of the pan. The flavor of this dish improves if you make it a day ahead of time and reheat it.

PER SERVING:
195 calories, 7g protein, 23g carbohydrates, 8g fat, 152mg sodium, 5mg cholesterol, 2.5g fiber

GREEN PEAS AND HOMEMADE CHEESE IN TOMATO SAUCE (MATAR PANEER)

*P*aneer is a homemade Indian cheese. While not yet available in conventional supermarkets, this product is readily available in Indian grocery stores. Directions for making it at home can be found on page 11. Paneer absorbs the flavors of garam masala, chili powder, and coriander. This dish goes well with any Indian bread, such as chapati, paratha, or nan—see Chapter 8.

PREPARATION TIME: *15 minutes* COOKING TIME: *45 minutes* SERVES: 4

FOR THE ONION–GARLIC PASTE:
1 onion, peeled and chopped
2 cloves garlic, peeled
1 inch fresh ginger, peeled and chopped
8 cashews
½ cup tomato puree

Paneer made with 4 cups 2% milk, or ½ lb. packaged paneer cubes (see note above)
Flour for dusting
2 Tbsp. vegetable oil
¼ tsp. ground turmeric

2 ripe tomatoes, chopped
2 cups fresh peas, cooked according to your favorite method, or 1 (10 oz.) package frozen peas, cooked according to package directions
¼ cup water
1 tsp. salt
¼ tsp. freshly ground black pepper
¼ tsp. chili powder
1 tsp. ground coriander
½ tsp. garam masala (p. 25)

2 Tbsp. chopped fresh cilantro

1. To prepare the onion-garlic paste:
In a blender or food processor fitted with a steel blade, process the onion, garlic, ginger, cashews, and tomato puree to a smooth paste. Set aside.
2. Dust the paneer pieces lightly with the flour to prevent spattering. In a large, heavy-bottomed nonstick sauté pan, heat 1 tablespoon of the oil. Add the pieces of paneer in a single layer and gently sauté them over medium heat until they turn a shade darker on all sides. Remove the paneer with a slotted spoon. Set aside.
3. In the same pan, heat the remaining tablespoon of oil. Add the onion-garlic paste and the turmeric. The paste can spatter, so be careful to keep your face a safe dis-

tance from the pan. Sauté, stirring constantly, for 10 minutes, until the paste turns golden. Add the chopped tomatoes, peas, water, salt, pepper, chili powder, coriander, and garam masala, and continue sautéing over medium heat for 10 minutes. Add the fried paneer and cook for 5 more minutes.

4. Serve hot garnished with the cilantro.

PER SERVING:
217 calories, 18g protein, 16g carbohydrates, 9g fat, 113mg sodium, 20mg cholesterol, 5g fiber

SPINACH WITH HOMEMADE CHEESE (SAAG PANEER)

*his has always been a favorite in our family. Fiber-rich spinach tastes great with homemade cheese. You can use either fresh or frozen spinach for this recipe.

PREPARATION TIME: *20 minutes* COOKING TIME: *45 minutes* SERVES: 4

Paneer made with 4 cups whole milk (p. 11), or ½ lb. packaged paneer cubes (available from Indian grocers)
Flour for dusting
3 Tbsp. light vegetable oil
2 onions, peeled, halved, and thinly sliced
2 cloves garlic, peeled and minced
1 inch fresh ginger, peeled and minced
1–2 green chilies or jalapeño peppers, stemmed and thinly sliced

1 lb. fresh spinach, thoroughly washed and stemmed, or 1 (10 oz.) package frozen spinach, thawed and squeezed dry
1 cup water
1 tsp. salt or to taste
¼–½ tsp. garam masala (p. 25)
⅛ tsp. cayenne pepper
4 Tbsp. half-and-half

1. Lightly dust the paneer pieces with flour to prevent spattering. In a heavy-bottomed nonstick saucepan, heat 1 tablespoon of the oil. Sauté the paneer pieces until they turn a shade darker on all sides. Remove them with a slotted spoon. Set aside.

2. In the same pan, heat the remaining 2 tablespoons of oil. Add the onions, garlic, ginger, and green chilies, and sauté, stirring constantly for 5 minutes over medium heat until the onions are soft. Add the spinach and water, and simmer until the spinach is wilted. Let cool. Pour the contents of the saucepan into a blender or the bowl of a food processor fitted with a steel blade, and process to a coarse puree.

3. Pour the puree back into the saucepan and add the salt, garam masala, and cayenne pepper, and simmer for 5 more minutes over medium heat until the flavors are well blended. Add the fried paneer and half-and-half, and gently simmer over low heat for 5 more minutes. Serve hot.

4. You can prepare this dish 2 days in advance, refrigerate, and reheat just before serving.

PER SERVING:
   180 calories, 18g protein, 10g carbohydrates, 7g fat, 160mg sodium, 7.5mg cholesterol, 2.5g fiber

MIXED VEGETABLE KORMA (NAVARATHNA KORMA)

Nava in Sanskrit means "nine" and *rathna* means "the finest." You don't have to use exactly nine vegetables—anywhere from five to nine will do—but do try to get the best of the season. The vegetables are simmered with ground spices and finished with a touch of cream. Serve this dish with any Indian bread (see Chapter 8) or whole wheat pita bread.

PREPARATION TIME: *15 minutes* COOKING TIME: *45 minutes* SERVES: 4

2 Tbsp. vegetable oil

2 onions, peeled and finely chopped

2 cloves garlic, peeled and minced

1 inch fresh ginger, peeled and chopped

½ tsp. chili powder

½ garam masala (p. 25)

¼ tsp. salt or to taste

3 ripe tomatoes, peeled and chopped

3 cups mixed vegetables (beans, peas, potatoes, carrots, cauliflower, red bell pepper, zucchini, asparagus, etc.), chopped and cooked according to your favorite method

1 cup low-fat milk

¼ cup half-and-half

2 Tbsp. chopped fresh cilantro

In a heavy-bottomed nonstick saucepan, heat the oil. Add the onions and sauté over medium heat for 3 minutes. Add the garlic and ginger, and sauté for 2 more minutes. Add the chili powder, garam masala, salt, chopped tomatoes, and the cooked vegetables, and simmer over medium heat for 15 minutes, until the sauce thickens. Add the milk and half-and-half and simmer for 2 to 3 minutes. Serve hot garnished with the cilantro.

PER SERVING:

180 calories, 6g protein, 17g carbohydrates, 9.5g fat, 145mg sodium, 8mg cholesterol, 2g fiber

VEGETABLE STIR-FRY

This is a vegetable dish with an Oriental flair. Serve it with Chapatis (p. 175).

PREPARATION TIME: *10 minutes* COOKING TIME: *25 minutes* SERVES: 4

2 Tbsp. vegetable oil
1 red onion, peeled and diced
3 carrots, peeled and diced
3 green or red bell peppers, seeded
   and diced
4 scallions, chopped
1 small cabbage, chopped
¼–½ tsp. cayenne pepper sauce

1 Tbsp. soy sauce
2 Tbsp. tomato sauce (can be
   canned)
½ tsp. brown sugar
¼ tsp. powdered ginger
¼ tsp. white pepper
Salt to taste

In a large nonstick saucepan or wok, heat the oil. Add the onion and carrots, and stir-fry for 5 minutes, until the onion is translucent. Add the bell peppers, scallions, and cabbage, and continue to stir-fry over medium-high heat for 10 to 15 minutes, until the vegetables are tender but still firm. Add the cayenne pepper sauce, soy sauce, tomato sauce, brown sugar, ginger, white pepper, and salt, and mix thoroughly. Turn the heat down to low, and cook, stirring, for 5 minutes more. Serve.

PER SERVING:
   125 calories, 3g protein, 12g carbohydrates, 7g fat, 269mg sodium, 0mg cholesterol, 2g fiber

MUSHROOM AND BELL PEPPER CURRY

*W*hite mushrooms and bright red bell peppers make this a colorful and tasty dish. Serve this dish with Chapatis (p. 175) or plain Parathas (p. 178).

PREPARATION TIME: *10 minutes* COOKING TIME: *25 minutes* SERVES: *4*

1 Tbsp. vegetable oil
2 cloves garlic, peeled and minced
1 inch fresh ginger, peeled and
   minced
4 red bell peppers, seeded and
   diced

1 lb. fresh mushrooms, diced
¼ tsp. salt or to taste
¼ tsp. cayenne pepper
3 Tbsp. tomato sauce (can be
   canned)
4 Tbsp. low-fat sour cream

In a large nonstick skillet or saucepan, heat the oil. Add the garlic and ginger, and sauté for 2 to 3 minutes. Stir in the bell peppers and mushrooms, and sauté over medium heat for 10 minutes, until they are tender but firm. Add the salt, cayenne pepper, and tomato sauce, and simmer gently over medium-low heat for 5 minutes. Before serving, fold in the sour cream.

PER SERVING:
105 calories, 4g protein, 11g carbohydrates, 4.5g fat, 187mg sodium, 5mg cholesterol, 2g fiber

SPICED GREEN PLANTAINS

*P*lantains, referred to as "cooking bananas," resemble bananas but they are larger and starchier, and unlike bananas, they must be cooked before eating. Sautéed and spiced, they work well as a sweet, tart side dish.

PREPARATION TIME: *15 minutes* COOKING TIME: *30 minutes* SERVES: 4

2 plantains
2 Tbsp. vegetable oil
Salt to taste
¼–½ tsp. chili powder

¼ tsp. ground cumin
¼ tsp. freshly ground black pepper
¼ cup low-fat plain yogurt

1. Peel the plantains and cut them lengthwise into four pieces; then cut the pieces into thin slices.
2. In a large nonstick skillet, heat the oil. Add the plantains and sauté over medium heat for 10 to 12 minutes, until tender and golden. Add the salt, chili powder, cumin, pepper, and yogurt, and simmer on low heat to prevent yogurt from separating. Continue to cook for 5 minutes, until the flavors have blended. Serve hot.

PER SERVING:
187 calories, 2g protein, 29g carbohydrates, 7g fat, 121mg sodium, 1mg cholesterol, 2g fiber

STUFFED EGGPLANT

*I*talian eggplants smothered in spices taste delicious.

PREPARATION TIME: *15 minutes* COOKING TIME: *35 minutes* SERVES: 4

2 Tbsp. vegetable oil	½ tsp. ground coriander
2 onions, peeled and finely chopped	2 tsp. brown sugar
1–2 tsp. curry powder	¼ cup cashews, finely ground
1 tsp. cayenne pepper	1 tsp. salt
½ tsp. ground cumin	8 Italian eggplants
	½ cup water

1. In a nonstick skillet, heat 1 tablespoon of the oil. Add the onions and sauté until soft. Add the curry powder, cayenne pepper, cumin, coriander, brown sugar, ground cashews, and salt, and mix well. Let cool and set aside.

2. Place each eggplant flat on a cutting board and cut it vertically in half. Cut each half from the top into four quarters halfway, leaving the bottom half uncut. Follow this procedure for the remaining eggplant. Fill a bowl with enough cold water to immerse the eggplant halves. Soak for 15 minutes. This allows the eggplant to open up slightly. Hold the eggplant half in your left hand and with your right hand take 1 teaspoon stuffing with a butter spreader and insert it into the slits. Fill the remaining eggplant halves with the stuffing.

3. In a nonstick skillet large enough to hold all the stuffed eggplants in one layer, heat the remaining tablespoon of oil. Place the eggplants in the skillet and add ½ cup of water, cover, and cook for 10 to 15 minutes over medium-low heat until the eggplants are tender. Carefully turn them now and then, making sure there is enough water in the bottom of the skillet to prevent them from sticking. Serve hot or warm.

PER SERVING:

170 calories, 3g protein, 17g carbohydrates, 10g fat, 111mg sodium, 0mg cholesterol, 5g fiber

ROASTED EGGPLANT IN TOMATO SAUCE (BAIGAN BHARTA)

*E*ggplant is oven roasted, then peeled, pureed, and mixed with spices and tomato sauce. Serve this dish with any Indian bread such as chapatis, pooris, or whole wheat pita.

PREPARATION TIME: *15 minutes* COOKING TIME: *45 minutes* SERVES: 4

- 2 large eggplants or 8 small Italian eggplants
- 2 Tbsp. vegetable oil
- 2 onions, peeled and finely chopped
- 4 cloves garlic, peeled and minced
- 1 inch fresh ginger, peeled and grated
- 2 green chilies or jalapeño peppers, seeded and minced

- ½ tsp. ground cumin
- ½ tsp. chili powder
- 1 tsp. salt
- 1 cup fresh peas, cooked, or 1 (10 oz.) package frozen peas, thawed and cooked
- 3 ripe tomatoes, peeled and chopped for ½ cup tomato sauce
- 4 Tbsp. half-and-half
- 2 Tbsp. chopped fresh cilantro

1. Preheat the oven to 400 degrees.

2. Prick each eggplant with a fork in two or three places. On a baking sheet lined with aluminum foil, arrange the eggplants. Bake for 30 to 35 minutes until the eggplants are tender and the skin begins to char. Let cool. Carefully peel away and discard the skin. Chop the pulp coarsely and set aside.

3. In a large nonstick skillet, heat the oil. Add the onions and garlic, and sauté for 5 minutes. Add the ginger and green chilies, and cook for 2 more minutes, until the onions are golden. Add the cumin, chili powder, salt, peas, and tomatoes, and simmer over medium-low heat for 2 to 3 minutes. Stir in the mashed eggplant, half-and-half, and chopped cilantro. Cook, stirring, for 5 minutes, until the flavors are well blended.

4. You can prepare this dish 2 days in advance. Refrigerate, then reheat before serving.

PER SERVING:
205 calories, 3g protein, 27g carbohydrates, 9g fat, 172mg sodium, 7.5mg cholesterol, 5g fiber

CHICKPEAS IN TOMATO, GINGER, AND GARLIC SAUCE

*C*hickpeas are flavored with fresh, aromatic garlic and ginger, and cooked with mild spices and tomatoes. This dish goes well with pooris, chapatis, any toasted bread, or plain rice.

You can always use dried chickpeas that have been presoaked and cooked (see instructions on page 159) for this recipe, but I've used canned here for convenience.

PREPARATION TIME: *10 minutes* COOKING TIME: *30 minutes* SERVES: 4

FOR THE TOMATO, GINGER, AND
GARLIC SAUCE:
1 Tbsp. vegetable oil
2 onions, peeled and chopped
1–2 green chilies, to taste
2 cloves garlic, peeled and chopped
1 inch fresh ginger, peeled and chopped
2 ripe tomatoes, peeled and chopped, or 1 cup canned tomato puree

FOR THE CHICKPEAS:
1 Tbsp. vegetable oil
2 (15 oz.) cans chickpeas, drained and rinsed, or 2 cups dried chickpeas, presoaked and cooked

¼ tsp. chili powder
½ tsp. ground cumin
½ tsp. ground coriander
1 tsp. brown sugar
¼ tsp. salt or to taste

FOR THE GARNISH:
1 onion, peeled and sliced into thin rings
1 ripe tomato, thinly sliced
1 Tbsp. finely chopped fresh cilantro

1. To prepare the tomato, ginger, and garlic sauce:
In a 3-quart nonstick saucepan, heat 1 tablespoon of oil and add the onions, green chilies, garlic, and ginger, and sauté for 3 minutes, until the onions turn golden. Empty the contents of the saucepan into a blender or the bowl of a food processor fitted with a steel blade. Add the tomatoes and process to a smooth puree.

2. To prepare the chickpeas:
In the same saucepan, heat 1 tablespoon of oil. Return the pureed sauce to the pan, and cook over low heat for 2 to 3 minutes. Add the chickpeas, chili powder, cumin, coriander, brown sugar, and salt, and simmer over low heat for 15 minutes, until the flavors are well blended. Set aside.

3. To prepare the garnish:
Coat a large nonstick skillet with nonstick cooking spray, and heat the skillet until hot but not smoking. Add the onion and keep stirring, and roast for 10 minutes, until it is deep golden and crisp.

4. Reheat the chickpeas and sauce mixture and serve with the garnish of crisp onion, tomato slices, and cilantro.

PER SERVING:
297 calories, 13g protein, 42g carbohydrates, 9g fat, 220mg sodium, 0mg cholesterol, 8g fiber

OVEN-ROASTED SPICED NEW POTATOES

These sweet, tender-skinned potatoes are oven-roasted with a blend of tangy spices.

PREPARATION TIME: *10 minutes* COOKING TIME: *1 hour* SERVES: 4

1 lb. small, white new potatoes
1 Tbsp. olive oil, divided

For the spice mixture (makes ½ cup):
1 Tbsp. cayenne pepper
1 Tbsp. ground cumin (or whole seed roasted and ground)
1 Tbsp. ground coriander (or whole seed roasted and ground)

½ Tbsp. ground fenugreek
1 tsp. ground cardamom
1 tsp. ground cinnamon
1 tsp. ground nutmeg
1 tsp. ground cloves
¼ tsp. ground turmeric
¼ tsp. freshly ground black pepper
¼ tsp. salt

1. Preheat the oven to 400 degrees.

2. Prick the potatoes with a fork once or twice. Grease a baking sheet with 1 teaspoon of olive oil. On the baking sheet, arrange the potatoes, pour the remaining oil on the potatoes, and set aside.

3. To prepare the spice mixture:
In a coffee mill or food processor fitted with a steel blade, process the cayenne pepper, cumin, coriander, fenugreek, cardamom, cinnamon, nutmeg, cloves, turmeric, and black pepper until the mixture is finely ground. This mixture stays fresh in an airtight container for 2 months.

4. Sprinkle 1 tablespoon of the spice mixture (more if you like it spicier) and the salt over the potatoes. Bake for 45 minutes to 1 hour, turning halfway through, until potatoes are fork-tender. Serve hot.

Per serving:
210 calories, 4g protein, 43g carbohydrates, 3g fat, 227mg sodium, 0mg cholesterol, 2g fiber

CHAPTER 6

RICE AND PASTA DISHES

....

SPICY FETTUCCINE WITH MIXED VEGETABLES

PENNE WITH CASHEWS IN HOT PEPPER SAUCE

ROTELLE WITH ONIONS AND GARLIC

SPAGHETTI WITH TOMATO-VEGETABLE SAUCE

LINGUINE WITH BROCCOLI

SPAGHETTI IN GINGER AND GARLIC SAUCE

RICE AND PASTA DISHES

RICE PREPARATION

Rice is classified as long, medium, or short grain. The long-grain rice is cooked until it is light, fluffy, and well separated, and is popular all over the world in preparing pilafs with fragrant spices.

The long-grain variety includes American Carolina, North Indian Patna, and the most popular, Indian basmati. Basmati rice is available in all Indian, Oriental, and specialty stores. Recently some of the American supermarkets have also started to carry this type of rice.

The short-grain rice, fat and oval, is popular in southern Europe and Southeast Asia. The dish most associated with short-grain rice in this country is Italian risotto. It is also used to prepare puddings and cakes.

The medium-grain rice is soft-textured and holds it shape when cooked. It is mostly parboiled.

CLEANING RICE

Regardless of the variety, always glance through the rice, picking out any foreign matter such as small stones, unhulled rice grains, and so on.

WASHING RICE

Use one of two methods: Place the rice in a large bowl and fill the bowl with luke-warm water. Rinse two or three times to get rid of the excess starch, until the water is clear. Or in a sieve, strain the rice under running water until the water runs clear. If you feel you need the vitamins that can be washed away with dirt and debris, use American packaged rice. You just rinse once and cook.

COOKING RICE

Stove-top Method Bring 2 cups of water to a boil in a heavy 2-quart saucepan. Stir in 1 cup of rice. Cover and simmer for 20 minutes or until the rice is cooked and all the water is absorbed.

Microwave Method In a 2-quart microwave-safe dish, combine 2 cups of water and 1 cup of rice. Cover and microwave on high for 20 minutes or until all the water is absorbed.

Electric Rice Cooker Method This is the easiest way. They come in various sizes: 2 cups, 5 cups, 8 cups, and so on. Wash and rinse the rice. In the cooker container, soak it for 5 minutes with the proper proportion of rice to water, then turn on the switch. It takes about 20 to 30 minutes, depending on the quantity of rice. For every cup of long-grain rice, use 1¾ cups of water. If using basmati rice, use only 1¼ cups of water for every cup of rice. Feel free to experiment with more or less water to make either moister or drier rice according to your personal taste. The biggest advantage to a rice cooker is that you do not have to watch the stove constantly or worry about the rice being over- or undercooked. These cookers are very durable and easily hand washable or dishwasher safe. If you eat rice frequently, it may be worth the investment for you.

Boiled Rice Wash and rinse the rice; soak for 5 minutes. In a large saucepan, boil water (1 cup of rice to 4 cups of water), and add the soaked rice and cook until tender, about 25 minutes. Drain like pasta in a colander or strainer, and transfer to a serving dish.

Baked Rice Wash and rinse the rice; soak for 5 minutes. In a large saucepan, boil water and add the soaked rice (1 cup of rice to 3 cups of water). Cook for 10 to 12 minutes, without stirring, until the rice is almost cooked but still quite firm. Drain the rice, then immediately transfer it to an ovenproof dish with a tight-fitting lid and bake in a 300-degree preheated oven for 15 to 20 minutes, until the rice is tender.

Fried Rice Wash and rinse the rice, soak for 5 minutes, and drain. In a heavy nonstick saucepan, melt 1 tablespoon of unsalted butter or ghee (clarified butter). Add the rice and gently sauté for a couple of minutes. For every cup of rice, add 1½ cups of water. Bring the water to a full boil and reduce the heat. Cover and cook for 20 to 25 minutes over low heat, without stirring, until all the water is completely absorbed and the rice is tender.

Steamed Rice Wash and rinse 1 cup of long-grain or basmati rice. Soak for 5 minutes. In a small pan, add the rice and 1½ cups of water and cover. Place this covered dish in a larger steamer pan and add enough water to surround the rice dish, making sure the water level is at least ¾ of an inch below the rim of the rice dish. As soon as the water comes to a full boil, cover the steamer pan, reduce the heat to low and cook for 20 to 25 minutes, until the rice is soft and evenly cooked.

Generally, 1 cup of dry rice yields 2½ cups of cooked rice.
Please note that recipe cooking times include rice preparation.

RICE DISHES

SIMPLE LIME (LEMON) RICE PILAF

In India they call this lemon rice pilaf, as lemon juice is commonly used to prepare the dish. I prefer the taste of lime, but you can use either lime or lemon juice. A pinch of turmeric added during cooking gives this dish a beautiful golden-yellow color, and the crunchy cashews lend a sweet delicacy.

PREPARATION TIME: *10 minutes* COOKING TIME: *45 minutes* SERVES: 4

1½ cups uncooked long-grain rice
1½ Tbsp. light vegetable oil
½ tsp. black mustard seeds
(optional)
1 tsp. split black gram (urad dal,
p. 161, optional)
¼ tsp. ground turmeric

2–4 green chilies, stemmed and
thinly sliced, according to taste
6–8 cashew nuts, chopped
2 Tbsp. fresh lime or lemon juice
¼–½ tsp. salt, to taste
3 Tbsp. chopped fresh cilantro

1. Begin cooking the rice according to your favorite method. Set aside.
2. While the rice is cooking, in a nonstick, 4–5-quart dutch oven or saucepan, heat the oil over medium heat. If you are using the mustard seeds, add them now, cover, and wait for them to sputter. Then add the split black gram and sauté until they turn a shade darker. Lower the heat and add the turmeric, green chilies, and cashews. Cook until the cashews turn golden. Turn off the heat.

3. Add the rice, lime or lemon juice, and salt, and stir well over low heat. Garnish with the cilantro and serve warm or at room temperature.

PER SERVING:
240 calories, 5g protein, 39g carbohydrates, 7g fat, 217mg sodium, 0mg cholesterol, 1g fiber

LIME OR LEMON RICE PILAF WITH PEAS AND ONIONS

The tangy flavor of this pilaf is mellowed by sweet peas and onions. It goes well with Tomato and Yogurt Salad (p. 84).

PREPARATION TIME: *10 minutes* COOKING TIME: *45 minutes* SERVES: 4

1½ cups uncooked long-grain rice
1 Tbsp. light vegetable oil
¼ tsp. ground turmeric
2–4 green chilies or jalapeño peppers, stemmed, seeded, and chopped

2 onions, peeled and finely sliced
½ cup fresh or frozen peas, cooked
¼ tsp. salt or to taste
3 Tbsp. fresh lime or lemon juice
½ cup chopped fresh cilantro

1. Begin cooking the rice using your favorite method. Set aside.
2. While the rice is cooking, in a heavy-bottomed nonstick skillet or dutch oven, heat the oil. Add the turmeric, green chilies, and onions, and sauté over low heat until the onions are just soft. Add the peas and a pinch of the salt. Cook for 1 minute longer. Turn off the heat.
3. Stir in the cooked rice, the remaining salt, lime juice, and cilantro, and mix thoroughly. Serve warm or at room temperature.

PER SERVING:
235 calories, 7g protein, 45g carbohydrates, 3g fat, 217mg sodium, 0mg cholesterol, 1g fiber

RICE PILAF WITH EGGPLANT

This version of rice and eggplant beckons with sultry curry flavors. The eggplant melds seamlessly with the rice and warm spices.

PREPARATION TIME: *15 minutes* COOKING TIME: *45 minutes* SERVES: 4

2 *cups uncooked long-grain rice*	½ *tsp. chili powder*
3 *Tbsp. vegetable oil*	½ *tsp. curry powder*
6–8 *small Italian eggplants, sliced*	¼–½ *tsp. garam masala (p. 25)*
into 1-inch-long, ⅛-inch-thick	2 *Tbsp. powdered, unsweetened,*
slices	*dried coconut*
¼ *tsp. salt or to taste*	1 *Tbsp. fresh lime juice*

1. Begin cooking the rice according to your favorite method. Set aside.
2. While the rice is cooking, heat the oil in a heavy-bottomed nonstick skillet or saucepan. Add the eggplant slices and sauté over medium heat for 6 to 8 minutes, until the eggplant softens but is still firm. Lower the heat.
3. Stir in the salt, chili powder, curry powder, garam masala, coconut, and lime juice. Simmer for 3 minutes. Add the cooked rice and stir. Serve warm or at room temperature.

PER SERVING:
   351 calories, 7g protein, 56g carbohydrates, 11g fat, 217mg sodium, 0mg cholesterol, 2g fiber

RICE PILAF WITH GREEN BELL PEPPER

The mild sweet taste of bell peppers is coupled with spices, creating a refreshing, simple pilaf.

PREPARATION TIME: *15 minutes* COOKING TIME: *45 minutes* SERVES: 4

2 cups uncooked long-grain rice
3 Tbsp. light vegetable oil
3 green bell peppers, seeded and
  diced into ¼-inch squares
¼ tsp. salt or to taste
½ tsp. chili powder

½ tsp. curry powder
½ tsp. garam masala (p. 25)
1 Tbsp. fresh lime juice
2 Tbsp. powdered, unsweetened,
  dried coconut

1. Begin cooking the rice using your favorite method. Set aside.
2. While the rice is cooking, heat the oil in a heavy-bottomed nonstick skillet or saucepan. Add the bell peppers and cook, stirring, for 5 minutes, until they are tender. Add the salt, chili powder, curry powder, garam masala, lime juice, and coconut. Stir over low heat. Stir in cooked rice. Serve warm or at room temperature.

PER SERVING:
335 calories, 6g protein, 53g carbohydrates, 11g fat, 215mg sodium, omg cholesterol, 1g fiber

RICE PILAF WITH FRESH DILL

Sweet basmati rice is combined with aromatic fresh dill and sautéed with hot peppers and minced garlic.

PREPARATION TIME: 15 minutes COOKING TIME: 45 minutes SERVES: 4

2 cups uncooked basmati rice
2 Tbsp. light vegetable oil
1–3 dried red chilies, cut in half
4 garlic cloves, peeled and thinly
  sliced

1 bunch fresh dill, washed,
  thoroughly dried, and finely
  chopped
½ tsp. salt or to taste

1. Begin cooking the rice using your favorite method. Set aside.
2. While the rice is cooking, heat the oil in a heavy-bottomed nonstick skillet. Add the red chilies and garlic, and cook for 1 minute. Add the chopped dill and sauté for

15 minutes, until the dill is wilted. Off the heat, add the salt and warm rice to the dill mixture, and stir. Serve warm or at room temperature.

PER SERVING:
295 calories, 7g protein, 51g carbohydrates, 7g fat, 215mg sodium, 0mg cholesterol, 3g fiber

RICE PILAF WITH CORN AND VEGETABLES

*his pilaf is a savory marriage of rice and vegetables. Spices give the dish an assertive flavor.

PREPARATION TIME: 20 *minutes* COOKING TIME: 45 *minutes* SERVES: 4 *to 6*

2 *cups uncooked long-grain rice (or brown rice, if you prefer)*
2 *cups water*
1 *(17 oz.) can corn, or 1 (10 oz.) package frozen corn or 1 cup fresh corn kernels*
2 *carrots, peeled and cut into 1-inch-long, thin strips*
2 *Tbsp. light vegetable oil*
¼ *tsp. ground turmeric*
1–2 *jalapeño peppers, seeded and thinly sliced, to taste*

1 *green bell pepper, seeded and thinly sliced*
3 *onions, peeled and thinly sliced*
3 *cloves garlic, peeled and minced*
2 *Tbsp. cashews, chopped*
2 *cloves*
2 *(1-inch) cinnamon sticks*
¼ *tsp. salt or to taste*

1 *Tbsp. chopped fresh cilantro*

1. Begin cooking the rice using your favorite method. Set aside.
2. Meanwhile, in a small saucepan, boil the water. Add the corn and carrots, and cook for 8 to 10 minutes, until tender. Drain and set aside.
3. In a heavy-bottomed nonstick skillet or saucepan, heat the oil. Add the turmeric, jalapeño peppers, bell pepper, onions, garlic, cashews, cloves, and cinnamon sticks. Sauté until the onions soften but maintain their shape. Turn off the heat.

4. Add the cooked vegetables and salt, and sauté for 2 to 3 minutes. Add the cooked rice and mix thoroughly. Garnish with the cilantro and serve warm or at room temperature.

PER SERVING:

400 calories, 10g protein, 70g carbohydrates, 9g fat, 235mg sodium, 0mg cholesterol, 4g fiber

RICE PILAF WITH PEAS AND GREEN BEANS

The special aromatic basmati rice makes this a delicious mild pilaf. If you cannot find basmati, use extra-long-grain rice instead.

PREPARATION TIME: *15 minutes* COOKING TIME: *45 minutes* SERVES: 4

2 cups basmati rice
½ cup fresh or frozen peas, cooked
1 (10 oz.) package frozen French-style green beans
2 Tbsp. light vegetable oil

3 onions, peeled and thinly sliced
2 (1-inch) cinnamon sticks
2 whole cloves
¼ tsp. salt
2 Tbsp. chopped fresh cilantro

1. Begin cooking the rice using your favorite method. Set aside.
2. Meanwhile, in a small saucepan, boil enough water to cover the peas and green beans, and cook for 8 to 10 minutes, until they are tender but firm. Drain.
3. In a heavy-bottomed nonstick skillet, heat the oil. Add the onions and sauté for 3 minutes, until the onions are soft. Add the cinnamon sticks and cloves, and sauté for 2 minutes. Add the cooked vegetables, rice, and salt, and mix well. Simmer over low heat for a few minutes to blend the flavors.
4. Garnish with the cilantro and serve warm.

PER SERVING:

339 calories, 8g protein, 61g carbohydrates, 7g fat, 107mg sodium, 0mg cholesterol, 5g fiber

RICE PILAF WITH CASHEWS, BLACK PEPPER, AND COCONUT

The black and white color combination of ingredients makes for a mildly sweet dramatic dish.

PREPARATION TIME: *10 minutes* COOKING TIME: *45 minutes* SERVES: *4*

2 *cups uncooked long-grain rice*
1 *Tbsp. light vegetable oil*
½ *tsp. cumin seeds*
1–2 *dried red chilies, cut into small pieces, or* ¼ *tsp. crushed red pepper*

¼ *tsp. freshly ground black pepper*
⅓ *cup cashews, halved*
Salt to taste
2 *Tbsp. freshly grated coconut*

1. Begin cooking the rice according to your favorite method. Set aside.
2. While the rice is cooking, heat the oil in a heavy-bottomed nonstick skillet or saucepan. Add the cumin seeds, red chilies, pepper, and cashews. Sauté for 2 to 3 minutes, until the cashews turn golden. Remove from the heat; stir in the cooked rice and salt. Serve with a sprinkling of the grated coconut.

PER SERVING:
308 calories, 8g protein, 53g carbohydrates, 7g fat, 110mg sodium, 0mg cholesterol, 1g fiber

RICE PILAF WITH CAULIFLOWER

This is a very mild pilaf with cauliflower cooked in a delicate blend of spices.

PREPARATION TIME: *10 minutes* COOKING TIME: *45 minutes* SERVES: *4*

1½ cups uncooked basmati rice or
   long-grain rice
1 Tbsp. light vegetable oil
3 onions, peeled, cut in half, and
   thinly sliced
2 jalapeño peppers, seeded and
   sliced

½ head small cauliflower, cut into
   ½-inch-thick slices and cooked
½ tsp. ground coriander
1 tsp. ground cumin
¼ tsp. salt or to taste
2 Tbsp. finely chopped fresh
   cilantro

1. Begin cooking the rice using your favorite method. Set aside.
2. While the rice is cooking, heat the oil in a heavy-bottomed nonstick large skillet. Add the onions and jalapeño peppers, and sauté over medium-low heat until the onions are soft. Add the cooked cauliflower, coriander, cumin, and salt, and sauté for 1 minute. Reduce the heat and stir in the cooked rice. Once the pilaf is warmed through, turn off the heat and garnish with the cilantro. Serve with plain yogurt.

PER SERVING:

267 calories, 6g protein, 53g carbohydrates, 3.5g fat, 222mg sodium, 0mg cholesterol, 1g fiber

YOGURT RICE

A cool, refreshing treat for a warm day. Creamy, fresh yogurt is folded into the mildly seasoned cooked rice, further enhanced by the distinct flavor of grated ginger.

PREPARATION TIME: *10 minutes* COOKING TIME: *45 minutes* SERVES: 4

1½ cups uncooked long-grain rice
1 Tbsp. light vegetable oil
1 or 2 green chilies or jalapeño
   peppers, seeded and chopped
1 inch fresh ginger, peeled and
   grated

1½ cups low-fat plain yogurt
¼ tsp. salt or to taste
2 Tbsp. chopped fresh cilantro

1. Cook the rice using your favorite method. Cool to room temperature and transfer to a serving dish.
2. In a small saucepan, heat the oil. Add the green chilies and ginger, and sauté for 2 minutes. Add to the rice. Stir in the yogurt, salt, and cilantro. Serve.

PER SERVING:
> 255 calories, 9g protein, 43g carbohydrates, 5g fat, 168mg sodium, 7.5mg cholesterol, 1g fiber

SWEET SAFFRON RICE WITH CASHEWS AND RAISINS

*S*affron, cashews, and raisins embellish this sweet-tasting rice dish.

PREPARATION TIME: *5 minutes* COOKING TIME: *45 minutes* SERVES: 4

1 cup uncooked long-grain white rice
¼ tsp. saffron threads
1 Tbsp. warm whole milk
1 Tbsp. melted ghee or unsalted butter

2 Tbsp. cashews, halved
2 Tbsp. seedless golden raisins or currants
⅛ tsp. ground cardamom
4–6 Tbsp. sugar or to taste

1. Begin cooking the rice using your favorite method. Set aside.
2. While the rice is cooking, place the saffron threads in a small bowl with the warm milk. Set aside to soak.
3. In a nonstick 2-quart saucepan, heat the ghee. Add the cashews and raisins, and cook over medium-low heat until the cashews turn golden and the raisins plump. Add the cardamom, sugar, and saffron threads with the milk, and stir until the sugar dissolves. Gently mix in the hot rice and serve.

PER SERVING:
> 240 calories, 4g protein, 45g carbohydrates, 5g fat, 0mg sodium, 7.5mg cholesterol, 1g fiber

RICE WITH SHREDDED MANGO

*T*here are two varieties of mangoes. Sweet mangoes are used for desserts, while "raw" mangoes are used for pickles and savory rice dishes. The raw mango is very firm with dark green skin and white meat inside; it adds a sharp, tangy flavor. This is a seasonal dish—raw mangoes are available in the warmer months.

PREPARATION TIME: *15 minutes* COOKING TIME: *45 minutes* SERVES: 4

1½ cups uncooked long-grain rice
1 Tbsp. light vegetable oil
¼ tsp. ground turmeric
2–3 green chilies or jalapeño peppers, stemmed, seeded and thinly sliced

1–2 dried red chilies, halved
½ cup peeled, shredded firm green raw mango
¼ tsp. salt
1 Tbsp. fresh lime juice
2 Tbsp. chopped fresh cilantro

1. Begin cooking the rice using your favorite method. Set aside.
2. While the rice is cooking, heat the oil in a heavy-bottomed nonstick skillet or saucepan. Add the turmeric and green chilies, and sauté over medium-low heat for 2 to 3 minutes. Add dried red chilies, sauté for 1 minute. Remove from the heat. Add the rice, shredded mango, salt, and lime juice, and mix well. Serve warm garnished with the chopped cilantro.

PER SERVING:
    228 calories, 6g protein, 42g carbohydrates, 4g fat, 110mg sodium, 0mg cholesterol, 1g fiber

RICE PILAF WITH CABBAGE

*C*abbage is shredded, simmered in mild spices, and mixed with rice.

PREPARATION TIME: *20 minutes* COOKING TIME: *45 minutes* SERVES: 4

1½ cups uncooked long-grain rice
2 cups water
½ cup fresh or frozen green peas
1 cup shredded cabbage
2 Tbsp. light vegetable oil
¼ tsp. ground turmeric
2 onions, peeled, halved, and thinly
  sliced
2 cloves garlic, peeled and minced
1 inch fresh ginger, peeled and
  finely grated

3–4 green chilies or jalapeño
  peppers, stemmed, seeded, and
  halved
Salt to taste
½–¾ tsp. garam masala (p. 25)
¼–½ tsp. chili powder or cayenne
  pepper
2 Tbsp. fresh lime or lemon juice

1. Begin cooking the rice using your favorite method. Set aside.
2. Meanwhile, boil the water in a saucepan. Add the peas and cabbage, and simmer
for 8 minutes, until they are tender. Drain.
3. In a 3-quart heavy-bottomed nonstick saucepan or large skillet, heat the oil. Add
the turmeric, onions, garlic, ginger, and green chilies, and sauté over medium heat
until the onions are soft but still hold their shape. Add the cooked peas and cabbage, and sauté over medium heat for 2 minutes. Add the salt, garam masala, chili
powder, and lime juice to the saucepan, and stir. Add the cooked rice and mix thoroughly. Serve warm.

PER SERVING:
270 calories, 6g protein, 46g carbohydrates, 7g fat, 218mg sodium, omg
cholesterol, 3g fiber

RICE PILAF WITH RED LENTILS, PEAS, AND PEARL ONIONS

The fast-cooking red lentils make this a wholesome dish.

PREPARATION TIME: *15 minutes* COOKING TIME: *45 minutes* SERVES: 4

½ cup split red lentils
1½ cups basmati rice
5 cups water
1 cup fresh or frozen peas
1 cup fresh peeled pearl onions or
frozen pearl onions
2 Tbsp. light vegetable oil
2 onions, peeled, halved, and thinly
sliced

2 cloves garlic, peeled and minced
½ tsp. salt
½ tsp. cayenne pepper
½ tsp. ground coriander
½ tsp. garam masala (p. 25)
½ cup finely chopped fresh cilantro

1. Rinse the red lentils and drain. Wash the basmati rice and drain. Cook the rice and lentils together with 3 cups of the water, using any method you prefer. Set aside.

2. Meanwhile, in a small saucepan, boil the remaining 2 cups of water. Add the peas and pearl onions, and cook over medium heat for 10 to 12 minutes, until they are tender. Drain and set aside.

3. In a heavy-bottomed nonstick skillet or saucepan, heat the oil. Lower the heat and add the onions and garlic, and sauté until the onions are golden. Turn off the heat.

4. Add the peas and pearl onions to the saucepan with sautéed onions. Add the salt, cayenne pepper, coriander, and garam masala, and simmer over low heat for 2 minutes. Add the cooked rice and lentils, and the chopped cilantro, and mix well. Serve warm.

PER SERVING:
   352 calories, 12g protein, 60g carbohydrates, 7g fat, 270mg sodium, 0mg cholesterol, 5g fiber

RICE PILAF WITH GARDEN VEGETABLES

*F*eel free to be creative in choosing vegetables for this pilaf.

PREPARATION TIME: *15 minutes* COOKING TIME: *45 minutes* SERVES: *4*

1½ cups uncooked long-grain white rice or basmati rice

3 cups water

2 cups fresh or 1 (10 oz.) package frozen French-style green beans

2 carrots, peeled and cut into 1-inch-long strips

2 cups fresh or 1 (10 oz.) package frozen peas

1 potato, peeled and cut into 1-inch-long sticks

2 Tbsp. light vegetable oil

2 onions, peeled, halved, and finely sliced

2 cloves garlic, peeled and minced

1 green bell pepper, seeded and cut into thin strips

2 dried red chilies, cut in half

1 tomato, chopped

1 Tbsp. plain low-fat yogurt

Salt to taste

½ tsp. garam masala (p. 25)

1 ripe tomato, sliced thin

2 Tbsp. grated Parmesan cheese

1. Preheat the oven to 375 degrees.

2. Begin cooking the rice using your favorite method. Set aside.

3. Meanwhile, in a 2-quart saucepan, boil the water. Add the green beans, carrots, peas, and potato, and simmer for 10 to 12 minutes, until tender. Drain, reserving the broth for later use.

4. In a heavy-bottomed nonstick skillet or 4-quart saucepan, heat the oil over medium heat. Add the onions and garlic, and sauté for 3 to 4 minutes. Add the green bell pepper, dried red chilies, and chopped tomato, and sauté for 3 minutes. Lower the heat and add the cooked vegetables, yogurt, salt, and garam masala, and stir well. Add the cooked rice and stir.

5. Grease a baking dish and add the rice mixture. Arrange the tomato slices and sprinkle grated cheese on top. Bake for 10 minutes. Serve hot.

PER SERVING:

358 calories, 10g protein, 59g carbohydrates, 9g fat, 133mg sodium, 2mg cholesterol, 5g fiber

RICE WITH RED KIDNEY BEANS AND VEGETABLES

If you have the time, prepare dried beans (see instructions on page *159*). You can also use canned beans for this recipe.

PREPARATION TIME: *15 minutes* COOKING TIME: *45 minutes* SERVES: 4

1½ cups uncooked long-grain rice
2 cups water
2 carrots, peeled and cut into thin quarters
1 (10 oz.) package frozen French-style green beans
2 Tbsp. virgin olive oil
2 onions, peeled, halved, and finely sliced

1 (16 oz.) can red kidney beans, drained and rinsed, or 1 cup dried red kidney beans, presoaked and cooked
½ tsp. cayenne pepper
¼ cup tomato sauce (can be canned)
Salt to taste

1. Begin cooking the rice using your favorite method. Set aside.
2. In a saucepan, boil the water. Add the carrots and green beans, and cook over medium heat for 10 minutes, until tender. Drain.
3. In a heavy-bottomed nonstick saucepan, heat the oil. Add the onions and sauté for 2 to 3 minutes over medium heat. Add the cooked vegetables, kidney beans, cayenne pepper, tomato sauce, and salt, and stir well. Simmer for 5 to 7 minutes.
4. On a serving platter, form the rice into a ring. Fill the center with kidney beans and vegetables. Serve hot.

PER SERVING:
399 calories, 12g protein, 72g carbohydrates, 7g fat, 600mg sodium, 0mg cholesterol, 6g fiber

RICE PILAF WITH MUSHROOMS

You can serve this pilaf with plain yogurt or any yogurt salad.

PREPARATION TIME: *10 minutes* COOKING TIME: *45 minutes* SERVES: 4

1½ cups uncooked long-grain rice
or basmati rice
2 Tbsp. light vegetable or virgin
olive oil
1 tsp. cumin seeds
3 onions, peeled, halved, and thinly
sliced

2 cloves garlic, peeled and minced
10 oz. fresh mushrooms, cut into
⅛-inch slices
¼ tsp. ground cardamom
2 whole cloves
½ tsp. ground cinnamon
Salt to taste

1. Begin cooking the rice using your favorite method. Set aside.
2. Meanwhile, in a heavy-bottomed nonstick saucepan, heat the oil. Add the cumin seeds, onions, and garlic, and sauté over medium heat for 4 to 5 minutes, until the onions are soft. Add the mushrooms, cardamom, cloves, and cinnamon, and continue to cook, stirring, until the mushrooms are tender, about 3 to 4 minutes. Add the cooked rice and salt, and stir.
3. If you wish, you can remove the cloves before serving.

PER SERVING:
   272 calories, 6g protein, 44g carbohydrates, 8g fat, 108mg sodium, 0mg
   cholesterol, 2g fiber

RICE PILAF WITH CILANTRO AND JALAPEÑO PEPPERS

You can make this dish as spicy as you like by adjusting the number of hot peppers.

PREPARATION TIME: *20 minutes* COOKING TIME: *45 minutes* SERVES: 4

1½ cups uncooked basmati rice
3 cups water
2 cups fresh or 1 (10 oz.) package frozen peas
2 cups fresh green beans, or 1 (10 oz.) package frozen French-style green beans
2 carrots, peeled and cut into 1-inch-long pieces

FOR THE CURRY PASTE:
½ cup fresh cilantro leaves
2–4 jalapeño peppers

1 inch fresh ginger, peeled
3 cloves garlic, peeled
1 inch cinnamon stick
1 whole clove
1 cardamom pod
¼ cup water

2 Tbsp. light vegetable oil
2 onions, peeled, halved, and thinly sliced
Salt to taste

1. Begin cooking the rice using your favorite method. Set aside.
2. Meanwhile, in a saucepan, boil 3 cups of water. Add the peas, beans, and carrots, and cook over medium heat for 10 minutes, until the vegetables are tender. Drain.
3. In a blender or food processor fitted with a steel blade, blend the cilantro, jalapeño peppers, ginger, garlic, cinnamon, clove, cardamom, and ¼ of cup water to a smooth puree. Set aside.
4. In a heavy-bottomed nonstick 5-quart saucepan, heat the oil. Add the onions and sauté over medium heat until golden. Reduce the heat, add the curry paste, and cook over low heat for 5 more minutes, until the paste thickens and you can smell the aroma of the spices. Stir in the cooked vegetables and salt, and after a few minutes, add the cooked rice. Stir frequently over low heat for 2 minutes.
5. Serve hot or warm.

PER SERVING:
332 calories, 10g protein, 55g carbohydrates, 8g fat, 122mg sodium, 0mg cholesterol, 5g fiber

VEGETABLE BIRYANI

*B*iryani refers to a combination of vegetables and rice cooked with a variety of spices. This is traditionally nonvegetarian, but this vegetarian version is very tasty, and the recipe lives up to its name.

PREPARATION TIME: *20 minutes* COOKING TIME: *1 hour* SERVES: *4–6*

1½ cups uncooked basmati rice
1 potato, peeled and cut into
  chunks
2 carrots, peeled and cut into
  quarters
2 cups fresh or 1 (10 oz.) package
  frozen peas
10 cauliflower florets

FOR THE CURRY PASTE:
1 Tbsp. grated fresh coconut
1–2 jalapeño peppers or green
  chilies
1 inch fresh ginger, peeled
3 cardamom pods

3 whole cloves
2 inch cinnamon stick
1 tsp. white poppy seeds, or
  6 whole cashews
1 tsp. coriander seeds
½ tsp. cumin seeds
2 cloves garlic, peeled

2 Tbsp. light vegetable oil
3 onions, peeled, halved, and thinly
  sliced
½ tsp. salt or to taste
2 Tbsp. fresh lime or lemon juice
2 Tbsp. finely chopped fresh
  cilantro

1. Begin cooking the rice using your favorite method. Set aside.
2. Meanwhile, in a saucepan, boil enough water to cover and add the potato, carrots, peas, and cauliflower, and simmer for 10 to 12 minutes, until the vegetables are tender. Drain and set aside.
3. In a blender or food processor fitted with a steel blade, blend the coconut, jalapeño peppers, ginger, cardamom, cloves, cinnamon, white poppy seeds, coriander, cumin, and garlic, until the mixture is smooth. Set aside.
4. In a large heavy-bottomed nonstick saucepan, heat the oil. Add the onions and sauté over medium heat until they turn golden. Add the curry paste and cook for 5 minutes, until you can smell the aroma of the spices. Add the cooked rice, vegetables, salt, and lime juice, and mix thoroughly.
5. Serve hot or at room temperature garnished with the cilantro.

PER SERVING:

> 350 calories, 10g protein, 60g carbohydrates, 8g fat, 235mg sodium, omg cholesterol, 6g fiber

VEGETARIAN PAELLA

*T*his is a mildly spiced, vegetarian version of the Spanish dish.

PREPARATION TIME: *20 minutes* COOKING TIME: *45 minutes* SERVES: 4

1½ cups uncooked long-grain white or brown rice

2 cups water

½ cup fresh pea pods, cut in half

1 cup fresh or 1 (10 oz.) package frozen peas

2 Tbsp. virgin olive oil

2 onions, peeled and chopped

2 cloves garlic, peeled and minced

10 cashews, split in half lengthwise

1 red bell pepper, seeded and chopped

1 green bell pepper, seeded and chopped

2 Tbsp. tomato paste

2 large ripe tomatoes, chopped

2 Tbsp. low-fat plain yogurt

¼ tsp. salt or to taste

½ tsp. cayenne pepper

1 tsp. garam masala (p. 25)

2 Tbsp. chopped fresh cilantro

1. Begin cooking the rice using your favorite method. Set aside.

2. Meanwhile, in a saucepan, boil the water. Add the pea pods and peas, and simmer over medium heat about 10 minutes, until they are tender. Drain and set aside.

3. In a nonstick 5-quart dutch oven or saucepan, heat the oil. Add the onions, garlic, and cashews, and sauté for 3 to 4 minutes, until the onions are soft. Add the bell peppers and sauté for 3 minutes. Stir in the tomato paste, tomatoes, yogurt, salt, cayenne pepper, and garam masala, and simmer over low heat for 5 minutes. Add the cooked rice, cooked peas and pea pods, and mix well. Heat through on low heat for 2 to 3 minutes.

4. Sprinkle with the chopped cilantro and serve.

PER SERVING:
340 calories, 10g protein, 56g carbohydrates, 8.5g fat, 130mg sodium, 1mg cholesterol, 5g fiber

PASTA DISHES

SPICY FETTUCCINE WITH MIXED VEGETABLES

I use frozen mixed vegetables here, but you can use any combination of fresh or frozen vegetables.

PREPARATION TIME: *10 minutes* COOKING TIME: *25 minutes* SERVES: 4

½ lb. uncooked fettuccine
1½ Tbsp. virgin olive oil
2 onions, peeled, halved, and thinly sliced
2 cloves garlic, peeled and minced
1 (16 oz.) package frozen mixed vegetables
¼ cup water or vegetable broth

½ tsp. chili powder
½ tsp. curry powder
¼ tsp. freshly ground black pepper
½ tsp. oregano
3 Tbsp. tomato sauce (can be canned)
¼ tsp. salt or to taste

1. In a large pot of boiling water, cook the fettuccine according to the package directions.
2. Meanwhile, in a large nonstick saucepan, heat the oil. Add the onions and garlic, and sauté for 3 minutes. Stir in the mixed vegetables and the water, and cook over medium-low heat for 5 minutes, until the vegetables are tender. Add the chili powder, curry powder, pepper, oregano, tomato sauce, and salt, and simmer for 5 minutes.
3. Drain the pasta. Toss with the vegetable mixture and serve hot.

PER SERVING:
305 calories, 13g protein, 49g carbohydrates, 6g fat, 280mg sodium, 0mg cholesterol, 1g fiber

PENNE WITH CASHEWS IN HOT PEPPER SAUCE

The sweet, nutty flavor of cashews mellows the chilies in this dish.

PREPARATION TIME: *5 minutes* COOKING TIME: *25 minutes* SERVES: 4

½ lb. uncooked penne pasta

¼ cup water

FOR THE SAUCE:
¼ cup cashews
*1–2 dried red chilies or ¼–½ Tbsp.
crushed red pepper*

1 Tbsp. virgin olive oil
¼ tsp. salt or to taste
*1 Tbsp. finely chopped fresh
cilantro*

1. In a large pot of boiling water, cook the penne according to package directions.
2. Meanwhile, prepare the sauce. In a blender or small food processor fitted with a steel blade, process the cashews, red chilies, and water to a smooth paste.
3. In a large nonstick saucepan heat the oil. Add the sauce and salt, and sauté over low heat for 3 to 4 minutes, until the sauce thickens. Drain the pasta and add it to the saucepan, stirring, for 2 minutes.
4. Garnish with the cilantro and serve.

PER SERVING:
280 calories, 10g protein, 42g carbohydrates, 8g fat, 280mg sodium, 0mg cholesterol, 3g fiber

ROTELLE WITH ONIONS AND GARLIC

You can make this pasta as mild or spicy as you like by adjusting the number of jalapeño peppers.

PREPARATION TIME: *10 minutes* COOKING TIME: *25 minutes* SERVES: 4

1 lb. uncooked rotelle pasta

1½ Tbsp. virgin olive oil

2 onions, peeled, halved, and thinly
    sliced

½ tsp. crushed red pepper

2–3 jalapeño peppers, stemmed
    and thinly sliced

4 cloves garlic, peeled and minced

½ tsp. oregano

½ tsp. chili powder

3 Tbsp. tomato sauce (can be
    canned)

Salt to taste

2 Tbsp. chopped fresh cilantro

1. In a large pot of boiling water, cook the pasta according to package directions.

2. Meanwhile, in a large nonstick saucepan, heat the oil. Add the onions, crushed red pepper, jalapeño peppers, and garlic, and sauté for 3 to 4 minutes, until the onions are soft. Stir in the oregano, chili powder, tomato sauce, and salt, and simmer for 2 minutes.

3. Drain the pasta. Toss with the sauce and serve garnished with the cilantro.

PER SERVING:

    270 calories, 8g protein, 48g carbohydrates, 5g fat, 240mg sodium, 0mg cholesterol, 5g fiber

SPAGHETTI WITH TOMATO-VEGETABLE SAUCE

*U*se your favorite pasta shape with this spicy vegetable sauce. You can serve it either hot or at room temperature.

PREPARATION TIME: *10 minutes* COOKING TIME: *25 minutes* SERVES: 4

½ lb. uncooked spaghetti

1½ Tbsp. olive oil

2 onions, peeled and chopped

2–3 jalapeño peppers, stemmed
    and chopped

1 green bell pepper, seeded and
    chopped

1 cup fresh or thawed frozen sweet
    peas

2 cloves garlic, peeled and minced

3 ripe tomatoes, chopped

½ tsp. oregano

½ tsp. chili powder

1 (8 oz.) can tomato sauce

Salt to taste

2 Tbsp. chopped fresh cilantro

1. In a large pot of boiling water, cook the spaghetti according to package directions.
2. Meanwhile, in a large nonstick saucepan, heat the oil. Add the onions, jalapeño peppers, bell pepper, and peas, and sauté for 5 minutes. Add the garlic, tomatoes, oregano, chili powder, tomato sauce, and salt, and simmer over medium heat for 10 minutes.
3. Drain the pasta. Toss with the sauce, garnish with the cilantro, and serve immediately.

PER SERVING:
   347 calories, 11g protein, 60g carbohydrates, 7g fat, 124mg sodium, 0mg cholesterol, 5g fiber

LINGUINE WITH BROCCOLI

Here, pasta and broccoli are sautéed in olive oil with herbs and spices. Jalapeño peppers add pizazz.

PREPARATION TIME: *10 minutes* COOKING TIME: *25 minutes* SERVES: 4

1 small head of broccoli	*6 cloves garlic, peeled and minced*
½ lb. uncooked linguine pasta	*½ tsp. crushed red pepper flakes*
2 Tbsp. extra-virgin olive oil	*½ tsp. oregano*
2 onions, peeled and minced	*1 Tbsp. chopped fresh basil*
2–4 jalapeño peppers, stemmed and chopped	*Salt to taste*

1. Cut the broccoli into florets. Peel the tender stalks and slice. In a saucepan, boil enough water to cover and cook the broccoli until it is tender. Drain and reserve the broccoli and the cooking water.
2. In a large pot, boil the broccoli water—if necessary, add more water—and cook the pasta according to package directions.

3. Meanwhile, in a large nonstick saucepan, heat the oil. Add the onions and jalapeño peppers, and sauté for 3 to 5 minutes. Add the garlic and red pepper flakes, and sauté for 1 minute. Stir in the oregano and basil, and sauté for 2 minutes. Add the cooked broccoli and salt, and sauté for a minute or so.
4. Drain the pasta. Toss it with the vegetable mixture and serve.

PER SERVING:
316 calories, 11g protein, 50g carbohydrates, 8g fat, 120mg sodium, 0mg cholesterol, 4g fiber

SPAGHETTI IN GINGER AND GARLIC SAUCE

inger adds a touch of the exotic to this pasta dish.

PREPARATION TIME: *15 minutes* COOKING TIME: *25 minutes* SERVES: 4

½ lb. uncooked spaghetti

FOR THE SAUCE:
4 Tbsp. tomato puree
2 cloves garlic
1 inch fresh ginger
2 dried red chilies or 1 tsp. crushed
   red pepper
2 Tbsp. chopped fresh cilantro

1½ Tbsp. virgin olive oil
1 onion, peeled and thinly sliced
1 red bell pepper, seeded and
   julienned
10 oz. fresh mushrooms, thinly
   sliced
1 pint cherry tomatoes, halved
⅛ tsp. mustard powder
12 oz. evaporated skim milk
Salt to taste

1. In a large pot of boiling water, cook the spaghetti according to package directions.
2. To prepare the sauce:
Meanwhile, in a blender or food processor fitted with a steel blade, blend the tomato puree, garlic, ginger, chilies, and cilantro to a smooth puree.

3. In a large nonstick saucepan, heat the oil. Add the onion and sauté for 3 minutes. Add the bell pepper and mushrooms, and sauté for 2 to 3 minutes. Add the cherry tomatoes, mustard powder, pureed sauce, milk, and salt, and simmer over medium-low heat for 3 to 4 minutes.

4. Drain the pasta. Pour the sauce over the pasta and serve.

PER SERVING:

281 calories, 9g protein, 50g carbohydrates, 5g fat, 115mg sodium, 0mg cholesterol, 3g fiber

CHAPTER 7

LEGUMES (DALS)

....

LEGUMES (DALS)

Legumes, or dried beans, peas, and lentils, were an often misunderstood and overlooked food until recently. In the United States, it was thought a decade ago that only health-food nuts ate legumes. But thanks to nutritional research, the Western world is learning more about the benefits of eating legumes. Loaded with protein, carbohydrates, vitamins, and minerals, and low in fat, legumes are extremely versatile and marry well with a variety of fresh vegetables and interesting spices. Most legumes are available in the supermarket, and any special varieties are available at health food stores, or Oriental or Indian markets.

If you are unacquainted with legumes, begin by experimenting with canned beans. For example, add chickpeas to a salad or combine split peas with rice, or create your own lentil soup and season with hot pepper to taste.

To prepare dried beans, follow the steps below:

1. Pick over the beans, removing pebbles, husks, and other debris.

2. Rinse them thoroughly in cold water. Discard any beans that float.

3. Soak them in lukewarm water for 6 to 8 hours or overnight, with the exception of split peas and lentils, which do not need soaking.

4. Rinse thoroughly two or three times before cooking.

5. Cook in fresh water—*never* cook in the same water as the beans were soaked in.

6. The beans can be then cooked in a pot with plenty of fresh water for 1½ to 2 hours or pressure-cooked in half the time. Split peas and lentils take only 45 minutes to cook on a stove top.

7. One cup of dried beans yields 2 to 2¼ cups of cooked beans (1 cup of dried beans = 16 ounces of canned beans).

8. You can presoak and cook more than you need. Store the excess amount in the freezer.

Quick-soak method:

Follow steps 1 and 2 of the preceding directions. Then, in a heavy-bottomed saucepan, add the beans and enough water to cover and bring to a boil. Boil for 2 minutes, remove from the heat, and set aside for 1 hour. Drain. Rinse the beans in fresh water and then cook as the recipe directs.

There are many varieties of beans to choose from. Here are the most common:

Aduki Beans Also known as adzuki and feijao beans. These are small, reddish-brown, oblong beans, native to the Far East, and great with salads and sprouts.

Black-eyed Peas Also known as cowpeas, they can be quick-soaked and cooked for 30 minutes. They are good for salads, stews, and curries. They have a firm texture with a mild flavor.

Chickpeas Also known as garbanzo beans, chickpeas are one of the most popular beans. They are readily available in cans or dried, and taste great in salads, sauces, and stews. They can also be roasted and ground into a fine chickpea or gram flour (besan), widely used by Indians to prepare savories and sweets.

Kidney Beans (Rajma) These are dark or light red beans. The most popular of the two are known as chili beans. They have a meaty texture and a sweet flavor.

Lentils Lentils are available whole or split and can be green, red, or pink. They are widely used for soups, salads, and stews. They make great-tasting low-fat dips and spreads. The split red lentils are used in rice dishes. The biggest advantage to lentils is they do not need presoaking and take only about 20 minutes to cook.

Lima Beans The larger lima beans are called butter beans, but the most widely used are the baby lima beans. Limas come fresh, frozen, dried, and canned.

Mung Dal or Mung Beans (Green Gram) Whole mung beans are best known in this country as sprouts or bean sprouts. Mung beans are available in Indian, Middle Eastern, or health food grocery stores. Split mung beans, with or without skin, are used for stews and sauces.

Soybeans Soybeans are used for tofu, soy milk, and sauces.

Split Peas Available in green or yellow, split peas need no presoaking, and they cook fairly quickly in about 45 minutes. They are readily available and are used for soups and vegetable stews.

Toovar Dal Also known as arhar dal or tuar dal, is used in soups, purees, and sambar. Toovar dal is rarely available in supermarkets but can be purchased in Indian or other Asian grocery stores. Yellow split peas can be substituted for this dal.

Urad Dal or Black Gram Urad dal is available whole, split with skin, or split without skin, and is sold mainly in Indian grocery stores. Masala dosa, a classic Indian dish, is made from split urad dal without the skin. This dal needs to be soaked for 4 to 5 hours and then pureed.

There are many other varieties of beans available in supermarkets—fava, great northern, pinto, navy, and others. Experiment with all of them, adding them to vegetable and pasta dishes, stews and salads.

· · · ·

BASIC TOOVAR DAL

*H*igh-protein dal is cooked, pureed, and mixed with spicy seasonings. Toovar dal and yellow split peas do not need presoaking.

PREPARATION TIME: *15 minutes* COOKING TIME: *45 minutes* SERVES: 4

¼ cup toovar dal or yellow split
   peas
4 cups water
¼ tsp. ground turmeric

FOR THE SEASONING:
   1 Tbsp. light vegetable oil
   ½ tsp. mustard seeds

1 tsp. cumin seeds
1 onion, peeled and chopped
4 cloves garlic, peeled and thinly
   sliced
¼ tsp. ground asafetida
2 dried red chilies or ½ tsp. crushed
   red pepper

Salt to taste

1. Pick over, clean, and wash the dal.

2. In a 3-quart saucepan, boil the water. Add the dal and turmeric, and cook for 35 to 40 minutes over medium-high heat, until the dal is tender. To test for doneness, squeeze a grain of the dal between your thumb and index finger. It should be tender. Turn off the heat. (This dal keeps for 3 to 4 days in the refrigerator and may be used for soups and sambars.)

3. With a wire whisk or a wooden spoon, beat the dal to a fine puree. Set aside.

4. In a small saucepan, heat the oil. Add the mustard seeds and cover. Reduce the heat and cook until you can hear the seeds spatter. Add the cumin seeds, onion, garlic, asafetida, and dried red chilies, and sauté until the onion is soft and golden colored. Add the seasonings and salt to the pureed dal, and heat through. Serve with rice.

PER SERVING:
   108 calories, 5g protein, 13g carbohydrates, 4g fat, 108mg sodium, omg cholesterol, 8.5g fiber

POTATO AND GREEN BEAN SAMBAR

The best way to eat dal is with vegetables, and this sambar recipe is a traditional combination.

PREPARATION TIME: 20 minutes COOKING TIME: 45 minutes SERVES: 4

*1 cup toovar dal or yellow split
   peas*
5 cups water
¼ tsp. ground turmeric
*½ pound fresh green beans,
   trimmed and cut into 1-inch
   pieces, or ¾ cup frozen green
   beans*
1 onion, peeled and chopped
*2 potatoes, peeled and diced into
   ½-inch cubes*
4 to 6 fresh curry leaves (optional)
*1–2 tsp. sambar powder
   (see pp. 210–11) or curry powder*
*½ tsp. tamarind paste; or 1 large
   tomato, finely chopped, plus
   1 Tbsp. lime juice*

*½ cup coconut milk or ¼ cup
   half-and-half*
1 tsp. brown sugar
¼ tsp. salt or to taste

FOR THE SEASONING:
2 tsp. light vegetable oil
½ tsp. mustard seeds
¼ tsp. ground asafetida

FOR THE GARNISH:
2 Tbsp. chopped fresh cilantro

1. Pick over, clean and wash the toovar dal. In a heavy-bottomed 3-quart saucepan, bring the water to a boil. Add the dal and the turmeric. Cook over medium heat for 30 to 35 minutes, until the dal is tender. Let it cool.

2. In a small saucepan, boil enough water to cover, and add the green beans and chopped onion. Cook for 10 to 15 minutes over medium-high heat, until the green beans are almost cooked. Add the diced potatoes, and cook until they are tender. Set aside.

3. With a wooden spoon or wire whisk, beat the cooked dal vigorously to a puree. To the dal, add the vegetables, curry leaves, sambar powder, tamarind paste (or the chopped tomato and lime juice), coconut milk, brown sugar, and salt. Simmer for 10 minutes.

4. To prepare the seasoning:
In a small saucepan, heat the oil. Add the mustard seeds and cover until you hear the seeds spattering. Turn off the heat. Add the asafetida, let the pan sizzle for a second, and then pour into the dal mixture. This seasoning gives a special aromatic, distinct taste to the dish. Simmer until the flavors are blended. Garnish with the chopped cilantro and serve hot.

5. Serve this sambar in individual bowls with steamed or boiled rice. This dish may be prepared a day in advance and reheated just before serving.

PER SERVING:
   260 calories, 10g protein, 34.5g carbohydrates, 9g fat, 220mg sodium, 7.5mg cholesterol, 11g fiber

NOTE: You can cook almost any variety of vegetables separately and mix them with the dal, then season and simmer until done. Here are some suggestions:

1. Yellow split peas (toovar dal) with kohlrabi and onions

2. Dal with red radish or white radish (Japanese daikon)

3. Dal with green beans and potatoes

4. Dal with spinach and onions

SPLIT PEAS WITH PEARL ONIONS, GARLIC, AND HOT PEPPER

Yellow split peas are cooked to a smooth puree, seasoned, and mixed with sweet pearl onions.

PREPARATION TIME: *10 minutes* COOKING TIME: *45 minutes* SERVES: *4*

*1 cup toovar dal or yellow split
    peas*
7 cups water
¼ tsp. ground turmeric
*1–2 dried red chilies, or ½ tsp.
    crushed red pepper, to taste*
*6 cloves garlic, peeled and thinly
    sliced*
*1 (16 oz.) package frozen or fresh
    pearl onions, peeled*
*½ tsp. tamarind paste; or 1 large
    tomato, chopped, plus 1 Tbsp.
    lime juice*

1 tsp. brown sugar
¼ tsp. salt or to taste

FOR THE SEASONING:
2 tsp. vegetable oil
½ tsp. mustard seeds (optional)
½ tsp. cumin seeds
¼ tsp. ground asafetida

FOR THE GARNISH:
2 Tbsp. chopped fresh cilantro

1. Pick over, rinse, and drain the dal.

2. In a 3-quart saucepan, boil 5 cups of the water. Add the dal and turmeric, and simmer over medium heat for 35 minutes. Add the dried red chilies and garlic, and cook until the dal is tender. Remove from the heat and beat the dal with a wooden spoon or wire whisk to a coarse puree.

3. In a saucepan with the remaining 2 cups of water, bring the onions to a full boil. Reduce the heat to medium, cover, and simmer for 10 to 12 minutes, until the onions are tender. Drain.

4. In the saucepan with the dal, combine the pearl onions, tamarind paste, brown sugar, and salt, and simmer for 5 minutes.

5. To prepare the seasoning:

In a small saucepan, heat the oil. Add the mustard seeds (if desired), cover, and cook until you hear the seeds spattering. Lower the heat. Add the cumin seeds and asafetida. The pan should sizzle for a second. Then add the dal and simmer until the flavors are blended.

6. Garnish with the cilantro and serve hot with rice. This dish can be prepared a day in advance and reheated just before serving.

PER SERVING:

198 calories, 11g protein, 33g carbohydrates, 2.5g fat, 227mg sodium, 0mg cholesterol, 10g fiber

SPICY BLACK-EYED PEA CURRY

You may substitute aduki beans for black-eyed peas in this dish, and any vegetable goes well, too.

PREPARATION TIME: *10 minutes* COOKING TIME: *45 minutes* SERVES: 4

1 cup black-eyed peas	*1 tsp. cayenne pepper*
2 onions, peeled and chopped	*½ tsp. ground cumin*
2 potatoes, peeled and diced into	*½ tsp. ground coriander*
1-inch cubes	*1 cup coconut milk or ¼ cup*
1 eggplant, cut into 1-inch chunks	*half-and-half*
1 tsp. curry powder	*¼ tsp. salt or to taste*

1. Soak the black-eyed peas in water for 1 hour. Drain. In a 3-quart saucepan, simmer the peas in 5 cups of fresh water to cover. After 25 minutes, add the onions and potatoes. Add the eggplant 5 minutes later. Continue to simmer for 5 minutes, or until all the vegetables are tender.
2. Add the curry powder, cayenne pepper, cumin, coriander, coconut milk, and salt. Simmer for 10 minutes until the flavors are blended.
3. Serve hot with rice, chapatis, or toast.

PER SERVING:
170 calories, 8g protein, 25g carbohydrates, 3.5g fat, 210mg sodium, 7.5mg cholesterol, 10g fiber

SPLIT MUNG BEANS WITH BELL PEPPERS

Mung beans are mild, easy to cook, and need no presoaking. You can substitute chayotes, also called vegetable pears or mirlitons, for bell peppers.

PREPARATION TIME: *10 minutes* COOKING TIME: *35 minutes* SERVES: *4*

1 cup split mung beans
4 cups water

FOR THE SEASONING:
1 Tbsp. vegetable oil
½ tsp. mustard seeds
½ tsp. cumin seeds
6 cloves garlic, peeled and thinly
sliced

2 green bell peppers, seeded and
cut into ¼-inch chunks
2–4 dried red chilies or ½ tsp.
crushed red pepper, to taste

1 cup coconut milk or ¼ cup
half-and-half
¼ tsp. salt or to taste

1. Pick over the beans and put them into a dry saucepan. Dry-roast over low heat until the beans turns a shade darker. Thoroughly rinse the beans and, in a 3-quart saucepan, cook them in the water over medium heat for 10 to 12 minutes, until they are tender.

2. For the seasoning:
In a saucepan, heat the oil over medium heat. Add the mustard seeds, cover, and lower the heat so that the seeds do not spatter. Then add the cumin seeds, garlic, and bell peppers, and sauté for 5 minutes, until the bell peppers are tender. Add the dried red chilies and stir to blend the flavors.

3. To the beans, add the seasoning, coconut milk, and salt, and simmer for 10 minutes. Serve hot with rice.

PER SERVING:
305 calories, 15g protein, 37g carbohydrates, 10.5g fat, 220mg sodium, 7.5mg cholesterol, 10g fiber

ADUKI BEANS WITH GARLIC AND TOMATOES

*A*duki beans do not need to be presoaked overnight, and they blend well with any vegetable.

PREPARATION TIME: *15 minutes* COOKING TIME: *45 minutes* SERVES: 4

1 cup aduki beans
1–2 dried red hot chilies
1 onion, peeled and chopped
3 cloves garlic, peeled and minced
1 large ripe tomato, peeled and finely chopped
½ tsp. salt or to taste

¼–½ tsp. curry powder
½ tsp. cayenne pepper
½ tsp. brown sugar
1 Tbsp. fresh lime juice
½ cup coconut milk or ¼ cup half-and-half

1. Pick over, rinse, and drain the beans. In a large saucepan, soak the beans in warm water and set aside for 30 minutes. Drain.
2. In a heavy-bottomed 3-quart saucepan, bring 5 cups of water and the beans to a boil. Add the dried red chilies, then cook over medium heat for 30 minutes. Add the onion, garlic, and tomato and simmer for 15 minutes, until the beans are tender and the onion is soft.
3. Add the salt, curry powder, cayenne pepper, brown sugar, lime juice, and coconut milk. Simmer for 5 minutes, until the flavors are well blended.
4. Serve hot with cooked rice or whole wheat pita bread.

PER SERVING:
    212 calories, 10g protein, 34g carbohydrates, 4g fat, 226mg sodium, 7.5mg cholesterol, 11g fiber

SPLIT RED LENTILS WITH SPINACH

Split red lentils (masoor dal) do not need any presoaking and take less then 45 minutes to cook.

PREPARATION TIME: *15 minutes* COOKING TIME: *45 minutes* SERVES: 4

½ cup split red lentils

4 cups water

1 (10 oz.) package frozen chopped spinach, thawed and squeezed dry, or 1 bunch fresh spinach, washed, trimmed, and finely chopped

1 Tbsp. vegetable or olive oil

½ tsp. cumin seeds

2 onions, peeled and chopped

2 cloves garlic, peeled and minced (optional)

1–2 green chilies or jalapeño peppers, thinly sliced, to taste

1 inch fresh ginger, peeled and grated

2 ripe tomatoes, finely chopped

¼ tsp. salt or to taste

½ tsp. brown sugar

1. Pick over, rinse, and drain the lentils. In a 3-quart saucepan, boil the water. Add the lentils and simmer over medium heat for 30 minutes. Add the chopped spinach and cook until tender.

2. In a nonstick saucepan, heat the oil. Add the cumin seeds, and when they turn a shade darker, add the onions and sauté until golden. Add the garlic, green chilies, and ginger, and cook for 2 minutes. Add the chopped tomatoes. Set aside.

3. Meanwhile, with a heavy spoon, beat the dal and spinach until coarsely pureed. Add the onion and tomato mixture, salt, and brown sugar, and heat through.

4. Serve with rice or chapatis. This dish may be prepared in advance and reheated before serving.

PER SERVING:

135 calories, 8g protein, 18g carbohydrates, 3.7g fat, 175mg sodium, 0mg cholesterol, 5g fiber

BABY LIMA BEANS WITH SPINACH

I've used frozen beans and spinach for convenience, but please substitute fresh if you prefer.

PREPARATION TIME: *10 minutes* COOKING TIME: *35 minutes* SERVES: 4

3 cups water
1 (10 oz.) package frozen baby
* lima beans*
1 (10 oz.) package frozen chopped
* spinach*
1 onion, peeled and chopped
½ tsp. curry powder

½ tsp. cayenne pepper
½ tsp. ground cumin
½ tsp. ground coriander
1 Tbsp. fresh lime juice
¼ tsp. salt or to taste
¼ cup coconut milk or half-and-
* half*

1. In a 3-quart saucepan, boil the water. Add the lima beans, spinach, and onion, and simmer over medium heat for 20 minutes, until the vegetables are just tender. Add the curry powder, cayenne pepper, cumin, coriander, lime juice, and salt, and simmer for 10 minutes. Add the coconut milk and heat through.
2. Serve hot with plain rice or with any bread. This dish may be prepared a day in advance and reheated just before serving.

PER SERVING:

138 calories, 8g protein, 22g carbohydrates, 2g fat, 266mg sodium, 7.5mg cholesterol, 6.5g fiber

RED KIDNEY BEANS WITH TOMATOES

*T*his combination creates a delicious curry packed with flavor and nutrition.

PREPARATION TIME: *15 minutes* COOKING TIME: *25 minutes* SERVES: 4

2 (15 oz.) cans red kidney beans
2 Tbsp. vegetable oil
1 onion, finely chopped
2 cloves garlic, peeled and minced
1 inch fresh ginger, peeled and
* minced*
1 tsp. ground coriander
½ tsp. ground cumin

¼–½ tsp. cayenne pepper
¼ tsp. ground cardamom
¼ tsp. ground nutmeg
Salt to taste
3 large ripe tomatoes, chopped, or
* ⅓ cup canned tomato puree*
½ cup plain low-fat yogurt

1. In a sieve, drain the beans and rinse thoroughly. Set aside.
2. In a large nonstick sauté pan, heat the oil. Add the onion and sauté over medium heat for 5 minutes. Add the garlic and ginger, and stir-fry for 2 to 3 minutes. Add the coriander, cumin, cayenne pepper, cardamom, nutmeg, and salt, and cook for 5 minutes. Add the chopped tomatoes and beans, and simmer for 10 minutes, until the flavors are well blended. Fold in the yogurt and serve with rice or bread.

PER SERVING:
216 calories, 10.5g protein, 27g carbohydrates, 7g fat, 107mg sodium, 2.5mg cholesterol, 10.5g fiber

CHICKPEAS AND PASTA WITH STIR-FRIED VEGETABLES

Choose your favorite vegetables and pasta shape (I've used rotelle) for this recipe. I've included a combination that I think works well.

PREPARATION TIME: *15 minutes* COOKING TIME: *25 minutes* SERVES: 4

1 (15 oz.) can chickpeas
1 Tbsp. extra-virgin olive oil
2 red bell peppers, seeded and diced
2 green bell peppers, seeded and diced
2 ripe tomatoes, diced
¼ tsp. crushed red pepper

¼ tsp. freshly ground black pepper
1 Tbsp. fresh lime juice
¼ tsp. salt
1 Tbsp. chopped fresh basil
1 tsp. oregano
½ lb. rotelle pasta, cooked according to package directions

1. In a sieve, drain the chickpeas and rinse thoroughly. Set aside.
2. In a large nonstick skillet, heat the oil. Add the bell peppers and stir-fry over medium heat for 5 to 7 minutes until they are tender. Add the tomatoes, crushed

red pepper, black pepper, lime juice, and salt, and cook for 5 minutes. Add the basil and oregano, and cook for 1 minute. Add the chickpeas and cooked pasta, and toss.

PER SERVING:
330 calories, 12g protein, 58g carbohydrates, 5.4g fat, 115mg sodium, omg cholesterol, 7.5g fiber

CHAPTER 8

BREAD

....

BREAD

The Indian breads—chapatis, parathas, and pooris—are made out of whole wheat flour and are not baked in the oven like American or European breads. We "bake" our breads on the stove top in a cast-iron skillet or griddle.

Indeed, it is an art to prepare these classic breads. In the beginning, making this bread appears to be a complicated process, but with a little patience and practice, anyone can master the technique. It is well worth the extra effort!

••••

CHAPATIS (WHOLE WHEAT FLAT BREADS)

Chapatis are the most popular of the Indian breads. Authentic chapati flour is available in Indian grocery stores, but you can substitute whole wheat flour (supermarket brands) for very satisfying results.

PREPARATION TIME: *5 minutes* COOKING TIME: *25 minutes* SERVES: 4 (MAKES 12 MEDIUM-SIZED CHAPATIS)

2 cups chapati flour, or 1 cup
whole wheat flour plus 1 cup
unbleached all-purpose flour
¼ tsp. salt (optional)
2 tsp. light vegetable oil (optional)
¾ cup plus 2 Tbsp. warm water
(95–100 degrees)

½ cup additional flour for dusting
1 Tbsp. melted ghee or butter,
vegetable oil, or olive oil to
brush on the chapatis

1. Into a bowl, sift the flour. (Add the optional salt and oil now, if desired, and stir.) Slowly add the water, gathering the flour to make a dough. Knead the dough in the bowl for 6 to 8 minutes, until the dough is smooth, soft, and very pliable. Press your index finger slightly into the dough, and if it springs back, it is well kneaded. Cover the bowl with plastic wrap or a lid and leave it in a warm place.

2. After 30 minutes, knead the dough for a minute then divide it into twelve equal balls. Dust them lightly with the additional flour to prevent them from sticking to one another, and return them to the bowl. Cover.

3. Heat a cast-iron or nonstick griddle or skillet on medium-low heat. Take a dough ball and flatten it between the palms of your hands. Dust it with flour on both sides and, with a floured rolling pin, roll it out into a 7-inch round. Keep dusting it with flour occasionally to prevent it from sticking to the work surface or the rolling pin. When the griddle is hot, gently place the chapati on the griddle and cook for 30 to 35 seconds until soft bubbles begin to form on top. Brush the top with a little ghee and flip the chapati and cook on the other side for 20 seconds. Remove to a platter and cover to keep warm. A well-cooked chapati should be light and fluffy. Cook the remaining eleven balls in a similar fashion, stacking them and covering them. Serve hot.

4. Chapatis can be prepared several hours in advance and then warmed before serving. Wrap them in foil and heat them at 300 degrees in a preheated oven for 10 to 12 minutes. Chapatis go well with any vegetable dish.

PER SERVING (3 CHAPATIS):
   256 calories, 8g protein, 40g carbohydrates, 7g fat, 107mg sodium, 7.5mg cholesterol, 8g fiber

CHAPATIS WITH CILANTRO

Fresh cilantro and hot peppers are pureed and folded into the flour.

PREPARATION TIME: *30 minutes* COOKING TIME: *30 minutes* SERVES: *4 (makes 8 chapatis)*

FOR THE CILANTRO PASTE:
½ cup chopped fresh cilantro
1–2 green chilies or jalapeño
peppers, stemmed, to taste
¼ tsp. salt
1 Tbsp. chickpea flour (gram flour
or besan)
½ cup water

FOR THE DOUGH:
2 cups chapati flour (or 1 cup
whole wheat flour plus 1 cup
unbleached all-purpose flour)
¼ tsp. salt
1 Tbsp. vegetable oil, or melted
ghee or butter

2 Tbsp. vegetable oil for brushing
½ cup additional flour for dusting

1. To prepare the cilantro paste:
In a blender or the bowl of a food processor fitted with a steel blade, combine the cilantro, green chilies, salt, chickpea flour, and water. Process to a fine paste. Set aside.

2. To prepare the dough:
Into a mixing bowl, sift the chapati flour. Add the salt and oil, and stir. Add the cilantro paste to the dough, and mix, forming a soft dough, adding a little water if necessary. Set aside for 10 minutes.

3. To prepare the chapatis:
In the bowl, knead the dough for a minute. Divide the dough into eight equal portions. Take one portion and form it into a round patty. Flour the work surface and both sides of the dough, and roll it with a floured rolling pin into a 7- to 8-inch circle.

4. Heat a cast-iron or nonstick griddle or skillet on medium heat. When the griddle is hot, put one chapati on the griddle and cook for 1 minute, until reddish-brown spots appear on the underside. Brush the top side with a little oil. Using a spatula, flip the chapati and cook for another 20 seconds. Brush with oil and remove from the griddle. Repeat with the remaining dough. Serve hot.

PER SERVING (2 CHAPATIS):
228 calories, 28g protein, 40g carbohydrates, 4g fat, 214mg sodium, 7.5mg cholesterol, 8g fiber

PARATHAS (WHOLE WHEAT FLAKY GRIDDLE BREADS)

PARATHAS

*P*arathas are triangular-shaped, fried flaky breads. Like chapatis, they are made out of whole wheat flour, but they are prepared using a slightly different method. The dough for parathas is oiled, rolled, and folded several times, giving this bread its distinctive flaky texture. The result is a bread crispy on the outside, soft on the inside.

PREPARATION TIME: *10 minutes* COOKING TIME: *30 minutes* SERVES: *4 (makes 8 parathas)*

2 cups chapati flour, or 1 cup whole wheat flour plus 1 cup unbleached all-purpose flour
¼ tsp. salt
1 Tbsp. vegetable oil
¼ cup water plus 2 Tbsp. warm water (95 to 100 degrees)

½ cup additional flour for dusting
2 Tbsp. oil to roll and brush the paratha
1 Tbsp. melted ghee or butter (optional)

1. In a bowl, sift the chapati flour and salt together. Add 1 tablespoon of oil and, using your hands, mix well. Slowly add the water to the flour to make a soft dough. In the bowl, knead the dough for 5 minutes, until it is very pliable. Cover and set aside in a warm place.
2. After 30 minutes, knead the dough for a minute and divide it into eight equal balls. Keep them covered to prevent them from drying out.
3. Taking one ball at a time, dust it with flour and make a round patty, flattening it on a floured work surface. Roll it into a 5-inch circle. Using a pastry brush, brush the top side with oil and fold the circle in half. Brush the top side of the semicircle with oil and fold it in half. Now the dough looks like a triangle. Flatten and dust the triangle with flour on both sides. Using a floured rolling pin on a floured work surface, roll the dough until the triangle measures 6 or 7 inches. Remove to a tray and cover to keep the paratha from drying out. Repeat with the remaining dough.

4. Heat a cast-iron or nonstick griddle or skillet over medium heat until hot. Taking one paratha at a time, fry for 1 minute, until brown spots appear on the underside. Using a spatula, flip the bread to the other side, adding ¼ tsp. of oil to the pan. Fry the bread for an additional 30 seconds, until brown spots appear on the flipped underside. (Brush the top with a little ghee or butter if desired.) Remove from the griddle and wrap in aluminum foil. Repeat the procedure with the remaining dough. Wrap the parathas in foil. Serve hot.

5. Parathas can be prepared several hours in advance. Just before serving, heat in a preheated 300-degree oven, wrapped in foil, for 10 to 12 minutes.

PER PARATHA:

129 calories, 4g protein, 20g carbohydrates, 4g fat, 53.5mg sodium, 7.5mg cholesterol, 4g fiber

ALOO PARATHAS (POTATO-STUFFED BREADS)

*hese parathas are stuffed with mashed potatoes and spices and served with any simple vegetable dish, buttered rice, or yogurt.

PREPARATION TIME: *30 minutes* COOKING TIME: *45 minutes* SERVES: *4 (makes 8 parathas)*

FOR THE DOUGH:
2 cups chapati flour or 2 cups whole wheat flour
1 cup unbleached all-purpose flour
½ tsp. salt
1 Tbsp. light vegetable oil
1 cup warm water

FOR THE STUFFING:
4 medium potatoes
¼ tsp. cayenne pepper
½ tsp. ground coriander

½ tsp. ground cumin
2 Tbsp. chopped fresh cilantro

Additional ½ cup flour for dusting
1 Tbsp. melted ghee or butter, or vegetable oil, for brushing the finished parathas

1. In a bowl, sift the flours and salt together. Add 1 tablespoon of oil and, using your hands, mix well. Slowly add the water to the flour to make a soft dough. In the bowl, knead the dough for 5 minutes, until it is very pliable. Cover and set aside in a warm place for 30 minutes.

2. Meanwhile, to prepare the stuffing:

Wash, peel, and cut the potatoes in half. In a saucepan, boil the potatoes in salted water to cover for 10 to 12 minutes, until they are fork-tender but firm. Drain, cool slightly, and mash. Add the cayenne pepper, coriander, cumin, and cilantro. Mix well and set aside.

3. To prepare the stuffed parathas:

Knead the dough for 1 minute and divide it into sixteen equal balls. Flatten a dough ball between the palms of your hands and flour it on both sides. On a floured work surface, roll the dough into a 6-inch circle. Set aside. Take another ball of dough and flour and roll it in the same manner. Take 1 tablespoon of the potato stuffing and spread it evenly on one of the dough circles, leaving a ½-inch border around the edge of the circle. Place the other dough circle on top and carefully press the edges of the circles together, forming a sealed sandwich. Reserve and keep covered. Repeat the procedure using the remaining dough, stacking the parathas with a piece of plastic wrap between each. Remember, as you are making your parathas, dust your work surface with flour from time to time to prevent the dough from sticking.

4. To make the parathas:

Heat a cast-iron or nonstick griddle or skillet over medium heat. When it is hot, put one paratha in the griddle and fry for 1 minute, until reddish-brown spots appear on the underside. Using a spatula, flip the paratha, adding a little oil to the pan. Fry the other side for 30 seconds. Brush the top lightly with ghee or butter. Remove paratha from the heat, wrap in aluminum foil, and reserve. Repeat with the remaining parathas. Serve hot.

5. Aloo parathas can be made several hours in advance. Before serving, heat in a preheated 300-degree oven for 10 to 12 minutes.

PER PARATHA:
218 calories, 6g protein, 36g carbohydrates, 4g fat, 109mg sodium, 3.7mg cholesterol, 5g fiber

On the following pages are additional stuffings for parathas that all use the dough and technique described in the Aloo Paratha recipe above.

GREEN PEA STUFFING

1 cup fresh or frozen peas, cooked
1 Tbsp. vegetable oil
2 green chilies or jalapeño peppers,
   stemmed and minced

½ tsp. ground cumin
½ tsp. ground coriander
¼ tsp. salt
1 Tbsp. chopped fresh cilantro

Mash the peas with the back of a spoon. In a sauté pan, heat the oil. Add the green chilies and sauté for 30 seconds. Add the peas, cumin, coriander, and salt, and sauté for 2 minutes. Add the cilantro and stir. Cool before stuffing.

PER PARATHA:
   164 calories, 4.5g protein, 24g carbohydrates, 4g fat, 160mg sodium, 3.7mg cholesterol, 5g fiber

CAULIFLOWER (PHOOL GOBHI PARATHA) STUFFING:

1 Tbsp. vegetable oil
1 inch fresh ginger, peeled and
   grated
1 small head cauliflower, grated

½ tsp. cayenne pepper
½ tsp. ground cumin
¼ tsp. salt

In a nonstick sauté pan, heat the oil. Add the ginger and cook for a minute. Stir in the grated cauliflower and sauté for 5 to 7 minutes, until it is tender. Add the cayenne pepper, cumin, and salt, and mix well. Cool before stuffing.

PER PARATHA:
   168 calories, 4.5g protein, 26g carbohydrates, 4.5g fat, 164mg sodium, 3.7mg cholesterol, 4g fiber

GRATED CARROT STUFFING

1 Tbsp. light vegetable oil
1 red onion, peeled and finely
   chopped
1 clove garlic, peeled and minced
1–2 jalapeño peppers or green

chilies, stemmed and finely
chopped
2 large carrots, washed, peeled and
   finely grated
¼ tsp. salt

In a nonstick saucepan, heat the oil. Add the onion, garlic, and jalapeño peppers, and sauté for 5 minutes, until tender. Add the grated carrots and cook for 5 to 7 minutes over medium-high heat, until the carrots are soft and lose their raw taste. Add the salt and stir. Cool before stuffing.

PER PARATHA:
> 155 calories, 4g protein, 23g carbohydrates, 5g fat, 167mg sodium, 3.7mg cholesterol, 4g fiber

CURRIED KIDNEY BEAN STUFFING

You can use either canned or dried kidney beans for this recipe. If using dried, see instructions on page 159.

1 Tbsp. olive or vegetable oil
2 red onions, peeled and finely chopped
2 cloves garlic, peeled and minced
1–2 green chilies or jalapeño peppers, stemmed and finely chopped
1 cup canned red kidney beans, drained and rinsed, or ½ cup

dried red kidney beans, presoaked and cooked
2 tsp. fresh lime juice
½ tsp. cayenne pepper
¼ tsp. ground cumin
¼ cup mild or hot salsa, according to taste
¼ tsp. salt

In a nonstick saucepan, heat the oil. Add the onions, garlic, and green chilies, and cook over medium heat for 5 minutes, until the onions are soft. Add the kidney beans, lime juice, cayenne pepper, cumin, salsa, and salt, and simmer for 2 to 3 minutes. The curry should be slightly dry. Cool before stuffing.

PER PARATHA:
> 180 calories, 5.5g protein, 27g carbohydrates, 5.5g fat, 160mg sodium, 3.7mg cholesterol, 6g fiber

VEGETABLE STUFFING

3 cups boiling water
½ cup fresh or frozen corn kernels
1 potato, peeled and diced
½ cup finely chopped cabbage
1 Tbsp. vegetable oil
1 onion, peeled and chopped
1–2 green chilies or jalapeño
*   peppers, stemmed and chopped,*
*   to taste*

½ Tbsp. fresh lime juice
½ tsp. ground cumin
½ tsp. ground coriander
½ tsp. garam masala (p. 25)
¼ tsp. salt
1 Tbsp. chopped fresh cilantro

1. In a saucepan with the boiling water, combine the corn, potato, and cabbage, and simmer over medium heat for 8 to 10 minutes, until the vegetables are tender. Drain.
2. In a nonstick skillet, heat the oil. Add the onion and green chilies. Sauté for 5 minutes. Add the cooked vegetables, lime juice, cumin, coriander, garam masala, salt, and cilantro, and simmer for 2 minutes. Cool before stuffing.

PER PARATHA:
   170 calories, 4.5g protein, 25g carbohydrates, 5.5g fat, 110mg sodium, 3.7mg cholesterol, 4g fiber

SPINACH (PALAK) PARATHA

This bread uses a slightly different technique. The pureed, cooked spinach is folded into the flour as the dough is prepared rather than stuffed inside the dough like in the preceding recipes. The result is a flakier, slightly more complex bread.

PREPARATION TIME: *30 minutes* COOKING TIME: *30 minutes* SERVES: 4 *(makes 8 parathas)*

*1 (10 oz.) package frozen chopped
 spinach, cooked, or 1 cup fresh
 spinach, cleaned and stemmed,
 cooked, thoroughly drained, and
 squeezed of excess water
¼ cup water*

FOR THE DOUGH:
*1 cup chapati flour or whole wheat
 flour
2 cups unbleached all-purpose flour*

*¼ tsp. salt
½ tsp. ground cumin
2 Tbsp. light vegetable oil
⅓ cup warm water (95–100
 degrees)*

*½ cup additional flour for dusting
1 Tbsp. vegetable oil, or melted
 ghee or butter, for brushing*

1. In a blender or food processor fitted with a steel blade, puree the cooked spinach with the water.

To prepare the dough:
2. In a mixing bowl, sift both flours. Add the salt, cumin, and 2 tablespoons of oil into a bowl. Slowly stir in the pureed spinach and mix thoroughly, adding a little water if necessary, until you have a firm dough.
3. To prevent the dough from sticking, apply a little oil to your palms and to the work surface. Place the dough on the oiled work surface and knead it for 10 minutes, until it is smooth and extremely pliable. Return the dough to the bowl, cover, and let rest for 30 minutes.

To make the spinach parathas:
4. Knead the dough for 1 minute. Divide it into eight equal portions. Take one portion and form it into a round patty. Dust it with flour and, with a floured rolling pin, roll it on a floured work surface into an 8-inch circle. Brush the top with oil. With a knife, make a slit in the dough from the center of the circle to the edge. Using your hands, roll the dough from the cut edge all the way around into a tight cone. Stand the cone up vertically. Compress the cone into a patty.
5. Dust it generously with flour and roll it into a 7-inch circle. Set aside, covered. Repeat with the remaining dough. Stack the dough rounds between sheets of plastic wrap to prevent them from sticking.

6. Heat a cast-iron or nonstick griddle over medium heat. When it is hot, put one spinach round on the griddle and cook for 1 minute, until reddish-brown spots appear on the underside. Using a spatula, flip the bread and cook the other side for 20 seconds. Brush the top with oil or butter and set aside. Repeat with the remaining dough. Serve hot.

7. Palak parathas can be prepared several hours in advance. Wrap in aluminum foil and heat in a preheated 300-degree oven for 10 minutes before serving.

PER PARATHA:
   120 calories, 4g protein, 20g carbohydrates, 2g fat, 107mg sodium, 3.7mg cholesterol, 4g fiber

NAN (LEAVENED FLAT BREAD)

*W*hen it is made commercially, nan or tandoori bread is cooked in a clay or brick oven. In this homemade version, nan is first cooked in a skillet then finished in a preheated broiler until it puffs. A spectacular sight!

PREPARATION TIME: *20 minutes* COOKING TIME: *30 minutes* SERVES: *4 (makes 8 nans)*

½ tsp. active dry yeast	*2 tsp. ghee or melted butter*
¼ cup warm milk	*¼ tsp. sugar*
2 cups unbleached all-purpose flour	*¼ cup low-fat plain yogurt*
½ tsp. baking powder	*1 Tbsp. ghee or sweet butter,*
½ tsp. salt	*melted for brushing (optional)*
½ tsp. baking soda	*½ cup additional flour for dusting*

1. In a small bowl, dissolve the yeast in the warm milk. Set aside for 5 minutes. In a large mixing bowl, sift the flour and baking powder. Add the salt, baking soda, 2 teaspoons of ghee, and the sugar to the bowl, and mix. Make a well in the middle

of the flour and slowly add the yogurt and yeast-milk mixture. Combine until you have a soft, pliable dough. Put the dough in a large bowl with enough room for it to rise and cover with a damp cloth. Set aside in a warm place for 3 to 4 hours.

2. After the dough has risen, knead for a few minutes, then divide it into 8 equal portions or balls.

3. Heat a cast-iron griddle or skillet and preheat the broiler.

4. Lightly flour the work surface. Flatten one of the dough balls between your floured palms. Using a floured rolling pin, roll the ball into a circle 6 inches wide and approximately ⅛ inch thick. Repeat with the remaining dough.

5. When the skillet is hot, sprinkle the top of the nan with a little water and put it on the skillet, top side down. Cover the skillet and cook over medium heat for 1 minute, until the nan puffs up. Using a spatula, flip the nan and place the skillet under the broiler for 1 minute, until brownish-red spots begin to appear on the nan. Remove the nan from the skillet and, if desired, brush with ghee or butter. Repeat the process using the rest of the dough. Keep the nan covered and serve hot.

6. These can be prepared 2 to 3 days in advance, cooled, wrapped in foil, and refrigerated. Just before serving, heat the foil-wrapped nans in a 300-degree preheated oven for 10 minutes.

PER NAN:
   140 calories, 4g protein, 24g carbohydrates, 3g fat, 112mg sodium, 6mg cholesterol, 1g fiber

ONION KULCHAS (LEAVENED FLAT ONION BREADS)

*L*ike nan, these breads are filling. You can use any onions for this bread—for a wonderful, sweet taste, make the kulchas with Vidalia onions, readily available in the summer months.

PREPARATION TIME: *20 minutes* COOKING TIME: *30 minutes* SERVES: *4 (makes 8 kulchas)*

FOR THE DOUGH:
1 tsp. active dry yeast
1 cup lukewarm water,
   approximately
2 cups unbleached all-purpose
   flour
½ tsp. salt
2 tsp. vegetable oil

FOR THE ONION STUFFING:
2 Tbsp. vegetable oil
4 onions, peeled, halved
   lengthwise, and very finely sliced
½ tsp. salt
¼ tsp. chili powder

½ cup additional flour for dusting
1 Tbsp. ghee or sweet butter,
   melted for brushing

1. To prepare the dough:
In a small bowl, dissolve the dry yeast in ½ cup of the lukewarm water. Set aside in a warm place for 10 minutes.

2. In a mixing bowl, sift the flour and salt. Add the oil and stir. Pour the lukewarm water with the yeast into the flour mixture and stir, using as much additional water as necessary to prepare a soft but firm dough. Put the dough in a bowl with enough room for it to rise and set aside in a warm place for 2 to 3 hours.

3. Meanwhile, to prepare the onion stuffing:
In a nonstick skillet, heat the oil. Sauté the onions over medium heat until golden. Add the salt and chili powder, and cook, stirring, for 1 minute. Remove from heat and set aside to cool.

4. To prepare the bread:
Knead the dough for 2 to 3 minutes and divide it equally into sixteen portions. Keep the portions covered.

5. Heat a cast-iron skillet or griddle and preheat the broiler.

6. Take two portions of the dough and, one at a time, roll them into balls and with your palms, flatten them. Lightly flour the work surface and, with a floured rolling pin, roll out each portion into a 6-inch circle. Evenly spread 2 tablespoons of the onion stuffing on one dough circle, leaving a ¼-inch border. With a little water, wet a ¼-inch border on the other dough circle and place it, wet side down, on the onion-stuffed dough circle. Press the edges together to seal the dough rounds.

7. Sprinkle a little water on top of the kulcha and place it, wet side down, on the hot griddle. Cook for 2 to 3 minutes until the kulcha puffs up. Put the griddle under the broiler for a minute until the kulcha has a few brownish-red spots on top. Re-

move the kulcha and brush it very lightly with the ghee or butter. Keep the kulchas warm, covered with a clean dish towel. Repeat the process with the remaining dough. Serve the kulchas hot with a curry of your choice.

8. You may prepare these breads 2 days in advance. Cool, wrap in foil, and refrigerate. In a 300-degree preheated oven, heat for 10 minutes before serving.

PER KULCHA:
  148 calories, 3g protein, 25g carbohydrates, 4g fat, 107mg sodium, 3.7mg cholesterol, 1g fiber

POORIS (DEEP-FRIED PUFFY BREADS)

*P*ooris are my favorite—their appetizing aroma and luscious taste are hard to resist.

PREPARATION TIME: *15 minutes* COOKING TIME: *30 minutes* SERVES: *4 (makes 20 pooris)*

> *1½ cups chapati flour plus ½ cup unbleached all-purpose flour, or 1 cup whole wheat flour plus 1 cup unbleached all-purpose flour*
> *¼ tsp. salt*
> *2 tsp. light vegetable oil*
>
> *¾ cup warm water (95 to 100 degrees)*
> *½ cup additional flour for dusting*
> *Enough vegetable oil for deep-frying*

1. In a mixing bowl, sift the flours and salt together. Add 2 teaspoons of oil to the mixture. Slowly add the water, a little at a time, and mix the ingredients into a soft dough. Turn the dough out onto a work surface and knead for 10 minutes, until the dough is smooth and very pliable. Put in a clean bowl and set aside covered for 30 minutes.

2. In a wok or deep-frying pan, heat the oil for frying over medium-high heat.

3. Knead the dough for a minute, then divide it into 20 equal portions. Keep the dough covered until ready to use. Take one portion and make a round patty, dust-

ing both sides with flour. With a floured rolling pin, roll it into a 4-inch circle. Repeat with the remaining dough, making sure the work surface, the dough, and the rolling pin are floured to prevent the dough from sticking.

4. The oil should be very hot (375 degrees). To test the oil, drop a piece of dough the size of a pea into the oil. If it floats, the oil is ready; if it sinks, the oil is not hot enough.

5. Slowly drop one poori into the oil. The poori will start to sizzle. Gently tap it with a slotted spoon, pushing it under the surface of the oil. Within seconds the poori will puff up and the underside will be slightly brown. Gently flip the poori with the spoon and cook it on the other side for a few seconds. Remove the poori and drain it on a tray lined with paper towels. Repeat the process with the remaining dough. Serve immediately.

6. Serve with any curry; I like Potato, Onion, and Green Pea Curry (see p. 98).

PER POORI:
    66 calories, 2g protein, 10g carbohydrates, 2g fat, 26mg sodium, 0mg cholesterol, 1.5g fiber

CHAPTER 9

UPPMA (CREAM OF WHEAT DISHES)

....

UPPMA (CREAM OF WHEAT DISHES)

In Indian cooking, cream of wheat, or farina, is first dry-roasted in a skillet (or today's cook can use a microwave) until crisp, then cooked with water and a combination of vegetables. Like its American counterpart, it is great for breakfast, but in my household we also eat it as a snack with tea or as a one-dish meal.

To dry-roast cream of wheat:
Stove-top method: Place cream of wheat or farina in a nonstick skillet. Dry-roast, stirring, over medium heat for 5 minutes, until it turns a shade darker. Let it cool.

OR

Microwave method: In a microwave-safe dish, dry roast the cream of wheat on high (100%) for 2 minutes, stir once, and dry roast 2 minutes more, until it turns a shade darker. Cool.

. . . .

UPPMA WITH CASHEWS AND ONIONS

Cashews add a crunchy, sweet taste to this great one-dish meal.

PREPARATION TIME: *15 minutes* COOKING TIME: *25 minutes* SERVES: *4*

1 Tbsp. light vegetable oil
1–2 green chilies or jalapeño
peppers, stemmed and sliced
thin, according to taste
5 cashews, halved
2 onions, peeled, cut in half
lengthwise, and sliced thin
2 cups water
1 Tbsp. fresh lime juice
½ tsp. salt or to taste

2 Tbsp. chopped fresh cilantro
1 Tbsp. melted ghee or butter
(optional)
1 cup dry-roasted cream of wheat
or farina (p. 193)

FOR THE GARNISH:
1 ripe but firm tomato, cut into
thick slices for garnish
1 cup low-fat plain yogurt

1. In a large nonstick saucepan, heat the oil. Add the green chilies, cashews, and onions, and sauté for 5 minutes until the onions are soft. Add the water, lime juice, salt, and cilantro, and bring to a boil. (If you are using it, add the ghee or butter now.) Reduce the heat to low, and slowly add the cream of wheat to the saucepan, stirring constantly in a circular motion until all the water is absorbed. Simmer over low heat for 2 to 3 minutes. If the uppma looks watery, simmer for an additional 2 minutes.
2. Serve hot topped with sliced tomato and a dollop of yogurt on the side.

PER SERVING:
    240 calories, 7.5g protein, 40g carbohydrates, 5g fat, 256mg sodium,
    12.5mg cholesterol, 2.5g fiber

UPPMA WITH SWEET PEAS AND PEARL ONIONS

*U*se fresh, sweet green peas in season for a flavorful dish.

PREPARATION TIME: *15 minutes* COOKING TIME: *25 minutes* SERVES: 4

2 Tbsp. vegetable oil
1 red or white onion, peeled and
  thinly sliced
1–2 green chilies or jalapeño
  peppers, stemmed and thinly
  sliced
2 cups water
1 (10 oz.) package frozen peas and
  pearl onions, or 1 cup fresh peas
  plus 1 cup peeled pearl onions,
  cooked

½ tsp. salt or to taste
1 Tbsp. fresh lime juice
2 Tbsp. chopped fresh cilantro
1 cup dry-roasted cream of wheat
  or farina (p. 193)
1 cup low-fat plain yogurt

1. In a large nonstick saucepan, heat the oil. Add the red onion and green chilies, and sauté for 5 minutes. Add the water, peas, and pearl onions, and bring to a boil. Lower the heat and simmer for 10 minutes, until tender. Add the salt, lime juice, and cilantro, and reduce the heat to low. Slowly add the cream of wheat to the saucepan, stirring constantly in a circular motion for 2 to 3 minutes, until all the water is absorbed.

2. Serve with a dollop of yogurt on the side.

PER SERVING:
    300 calories, 10g protein, 48g carbohydrates, 7g fat, 300mg sodium, 5mg cholesterol, 6g fiber

UPPMA WITH MIXED VEGETABLES

This is a colorful, satisfying dish that captures the freshness and flavor of a variety of vegetables.

PREPARATION TIME: 20 minutes COOKING TIME: 25 minutes SERVES: 4

2 Tbsp. vegetable oil

1–2 green chilies or jalapeño peppers, stemmed and thinly sliced

1 onion, peeled and thinly sliced

1 carrot, peeled and grated

1 green or red bell pepper, seeded and chopped

1 Italian eggplant, cut in half lengthwise and thinly sliced (optional)

1 potato, peeled and cut into ½-inch-long and ⅛-inch-thick chunks

2 cups water

1 cup fresh or frozen peas, cooked

1 ripe tomato, chopped

1 Tbsp. fresh lime juice

¼ tsp. brown sugar

½ tsp. salt

2 Tbsp. chopped fresh cilantro

1 Tbsp. melted ghee or butter (optional)

1 cup dry-roasted cream of wheat or farina (p. 193)

1 cup low-fat plain yogurt

1. In a large nonstick skillet or saucepan, heat the oil. Add the green chilies, onion, carrot, bell pepper, eggplant (if desired), and potato, and sauté over medium heat for 5 minutes, until the vegetables are tender. Add the water, peas, tomato, lime juice, brown sugar, salt, and cilantro (and ghee or butter if desired), and bring to a boil. Reduce the heat to low, and slowly add the cream of wheat to the saucepan, stirring constantly in a circular motion. Stir until all the water is absorbed. Simmer for 2 more minutes.

2. Serve with a dollop of yogurt on the side.

PER SERVING:

312 calories, 8g protein, 45g carbohydrates, 11g fat, 294mg sodium, 12.5mg cholesterol, 3g fiber

VERMICELLI UPPMA

Here's a wonderful variation: dry-roasted pasta!

PREPARATION TIME: *15 minutes* COOKING TIME: *25 minutes* SERVES: 4

2 Tbsp. vegetable oil

2 cups uncooked broken vermicelli

1 tsp. salt, to taste

8 cashews, chopped

¼ tsp. ground turmeric

2 onions, peeled and chopped

1–2 hot green chilies or jalapeño peppers, stemmed, seeded, and minced

1 green bell pepper, seeded and chopped

2 carrots, peeled and grated

1 Tbsp. fresh lime or lemon juice

2 Tbsp. chopped fresh cilantro

1 cup low-fat plain yogurt

1. In a skillet, heat 1 teaspoon of the oil and the vermicelli. Roast until golden. In a saucepan, bring 5 cups of water to the boil; add a teaspoon of oil, a quarter teaspoon of the salt, and the roasted vermicelli. Cook until the pasta is tender yet firm to the bite. Drain and set aside.

2. Meanwhile, in a nonstick 4-quart saucepan, heat the remaining oil. Add the chopped cashews, turmeric, onions, green chilies, bell pepper, and carrots. Sauté over medium heat for 10 minutes, until the vegetables are tender. Add the remaining salt, lime juice, and the cooked vermicelli, and simmer on low for 2 minutes more.

3. Garnish with cilantro and serve hot with a dollop of yogurt on the side.

PER SERVING:

360 calories, 11g protein, 56g carbohydrates, 10g fat, 270mg sodium, 5mg cholesterol, 2.5g fiber

TAPIOCA UPPMA

⚜

This dish is perfect for a light snack. To prepare tapioca for cooking, presoak it in lukewarm water for 1 hour, then drain.

PREPARATION TIME: *15 minutes* COOKING TIME *20 minutes* SERVES: 4

2 Tbsp. vegetable oil
1–2 green chilies or jalapeño
  peppers, stemmed, seeded, and
  minced
2 onions, peeled and finely
  chopped

8 cashews, coarsely chopped
2 cups presoaked tapioca
1 tsp. salt
2 Tbsp. fresh lime juice
2 Tbsp. chopped fresh cilantro

In a nonstick 3-quart saucepan, heat the oil. Add the green chilies, onions, and cashews, and sauté until the onions are soft. Add the tapioca and sauté for 2 minutes more. Add the salt, lime juice, and cilantro, and heat through. Serve hot.

PER SERVING:

  357 calories, 4g protein, 65g carbohydrates, 9g fat, 215mg sodium, omg cholesterol, 1g fiber

BREAD UPPMA

Green chilies add a little kick to this dish.

PREPARATION TIME: *15 minutes* COOKING TIME: *20 minutes* SERVES: 4

1 loaf soft whole wheat or white
  bread, sliced
2 Tbsp. vegetable or olive oil
2–4 green chilies or jalapeño
  peppers, stemmed, seeded, and
  minced
4 cashews, coarsely chopped
4 onions, peeled, cut in half
  lengthwise, and thinly sliced

2 cloves garlic, peeled and minced
1 inch fresh ginger, peeled and
  minced
2 ripe tomatoes, finely chopped
½ tsp. curry powder
½ tsp. salt
¼ tsp. brown sugar
2 Tbsp. chopped fresh cilantro

1. Cut the bread slices into 1-inch squares. Set aside.
2. In a nonstick 3-quart saucepan, heat the oil. Add the chilies, cashews, onions, garlic, and ginger, and sauté until the onions are golden. Add the tomatoes, curry

powder, salt, and brown sugar, and cook until the moisture is evaporated. Add the bread pieces and chopped cilantro, and cook, stirring, over medium-low heat for 2 minutes. Serve hot.

PER SERVING:
337 calories, 14g protein, 50g carbohydrates, 9g fat, 255mg sodium, 0mg cholesterol, 5.5g fiber

CHAPTER 10

DOSAS AND IDLIS

....

DOSAS AND IDLIS

DOSAS OR INDIAN CREPES

*D*osas are a traditional dish of southern India. Similar to the French crepe, dosas are usually served for breakfast but are perfectly suitable for lunch. It is an art to prepare a dosa, but not a difficult one to master and well worth the effort.

••••

PLAIN DOSA

*P*repare the batter a day in advance; use it as a master recipe for preparing dosas.

PREPARATION TIME: *20 minutes*   COOKING TIME: *45 minutes*   SERVES: *4–6* *(makes 16 dosas)*

FOR THE BATTER:
½ cup urad dal (p. 161)
2½ cups rice flour or rice powder
½ tsp. salt

3 Tbsp. vegetable oil

1 Tbsp. melted ghee or butter (optional)

1. Pick over and rinse the urad dal, then soak it in a bowl with 5 cups of water for 5 hours. Drain the dal and put it in a blender or food processor fitted with a steel blade. Add 1 cup of water and process to a smooth puree, stopping the machine occasionally to push the dal down into the blade with a spatula. Keep processing until the dal is ground into a very fine, fluffy batter. Set aside.

2. In a 6-quart stainless-steel dutch oven or pot with a lid, or any large container that will allow the batter to rise, combine the rice flour and salt. Slowly add 2 cups of water to the rice flour, mixing thoroughly to prevent lumps. Add the urad dal

puree to the rice flour, and mix well. Cover and leave in a warm place to rise for 20 to 24 hours.

3. After the batter has set, stir it thoroughly.

4. Heat a nonstick skillet over medium heat and pour a ladleful—about ½ cup—of batter into the middle of the skillet. Using the bottom of the ladle, gently but quickly smooth the batter outward in a continuous circular motion until the batter measures approximately 8 inches in diameter and is the thickness of a crepe. Add ¼ teaspoon oil around the edge and on top of the dosa. Cook over medium-high heat for 1 minute, until the bottom of the dosa turns a nice golden red color.

5. With a spatula, turn the dosa over and continue cooking on the other side for 30 seconds. Put the cooked dosa on a plate (drizzle with melted ghee or butter, if desired). Continue with the rest of the batter. Serve hot with a chutney of your choice (see Chapter 1).

PER DOSA:

135 calories, 3g protein, 24g carbohydrates, 3g fat, 54mg sodium, 2mg cholesterol, 0.5g fiber

MASALA DOSA

A masala dosa is made with the same batter and technique as the plain dosa but has a stuffing of chutney and potato curry.

PREPARATION TIME: *1 hour* COOKING TIME: *45 minutes* SERVES: *4–6*

FOR THE POTATO CURRY:
6 potatoes, peeled and cubed
2 Tbsp. vegetable oil
½ tsp. mustard seeds
½ tsp. ground turmeric
1–2 green chilies or jalapeño
    peppers, stemmed and thinly
    sliced
2 onions, peeled and thinly sliced

½ tsp. salt, or to taste
1 Tbsp. fresh lime juice
2 Tbsp. chopped fresh cilantro

Fresh Coconut, Fresh Cilantro, and
    Tamarind Chutney (p. 16)

2 Tbsp. melted ghee or butter to
    brush the dosa

1. Prepare the dosa batter as in the master recipe (p. 203) a day in advance.

2. In a saucepan, boil enough water to cover the potato cubes and simmer for 10 to 12 minutes, until the potatoes are tender, but firm. Drain and set aside.

3. In a 3-quart nonstick saucepan over medium heat, heat the oil. Add the mustard seeds and cover. As soon as you hear the seeds sputtering, lower the heat and add the turmeric, green chilies, and onions. Sauté over medium heat for 8 to 10 minutes, until the onions are soft. Add the potatoes, salt, and lime juice; mix well and simmer on low for 2 minutes. Mix in the chopped cilantro. Set aside.

4. Prepare the chutney and set aside.

To prepare the masala dosa:

5. Follow the master recipe for cooking the dosa until the underside of the dosa has a golden-red color. Reduce the heat and spread 2 teaspoons of chutney evenly over the top of the dosa. Then spread 2 tablespoons of the potato curry over half the dosa. Fold the other half over the potato half of the dosa, forming a semicircle. Dribble ½ teaspoon of ghee or melted butter on top of the dosa and serve immediately.

A NOTE OF PERSONAL PREFERENCE: Some people prefer serving the chutney on the side, but I like it cooked inside the dosa.

PER MASALA DOSA:
185 calories, 4g protein, 31g carbohydrates, 5g fat, 110mg sodium, 5mg cholesterol, 1g fiber

PLAIN UTHAPPAMS

An uthappam is much thicker than a dosa, more like an American pancake than a French crepe. You can make it soft or crispy, according to your personal preference. Prepare the batter one day in advance.

PREPARATION TIME: *15 minutes* COOKING TIME: *30 minutes* SERVES: 4–6 (*makes 12 uthappams*)

FOR THE BATTER:
½ cup urad dal (p. 161)
2½ cups long-grain rice
2¼ cups water, divided

½ tsp. salt

¼ cup vegetable oil for the griddle

1. Pick over and rinse the urad dal. In a bowl, soak it with 5 cups of water for 5 hours. In a separate bowl with 4 cups of water, soak the rice for 5 hours. Drain the rice and the dal. In a blender or food processor fitted with a steel blade, process the dal and ¾ cup of water to a smooth paste. Pour the paste into a dutch oven or pot with a lid or any container large enough for the batter to rise. In a blender or food processor fitted with a steel blade, process the rice and 1½ cups of water to a coarse paste. Add the rice puree to the dal puree. Add the salt and just enough water to make a thick batter, like the consistency of pancake batter. Set aside in a warm place for 16 to 20 hours or overnight.

2. Heat a nonstick griddle over medium heat and add 1½ ladlefuls, or ¾ cup, of batter in the center of the griddle, spreading the batter gently but quickly with the back of the ladle into a 7- to 8-inch circle. Drizzle ¼ teaspoon oil on top and around the uthappam. Cook for 1½ minutes, until the bottom is reddish-gold. Flip the uthappam and cook for 30 seconds on the other side. Serve hot with any chutney (see Chapter 1) and Sambar (p. 210).

PER UTHAPPAM:
176 calories, 4g protein, 31g carbohydrates, 4g fat, 90mg sodium, 0mg cholesterol, 0.8g fiber

VEGETABLE UTHAPPAMS

*U*thappams are delicious plain or with your choice of vegetables. Follow the master recipe for preparing the uthappam and add chopped vegetables to the batter just before cooking.

Here are some ingredient suggestions:

ONION AND PEA UTHAPPAM

2 large onions, peeled and very
   thinly sliced
½ cup fresh or frozen peas, cooked

¼ cup fresh chopped fresh cilantro
¼ tsp. salt, or to taste

ONION AND HOT CHILI UTHAPPAM

4 onions, peeled and finely sliced
2–8 green chilies or jalapeño
   peppers, stemmed and thinly
   sliced

¼ cup finely chopped fresh cilantro
¼ tsp. salt, or to taste

TOMATO AND PEA UTHAPPAM

2 ripe tomatoes, finely chopped
½ cup fresh or frozen peas, cooked
¼ cup finely chopped fresh cilantro
¼ tsp. salt, or to taste

ONION, SCALLION, AND TOMATO UTHAPPAM

1 onion, peeled and finely chopped
1 bunch scallions, white and green
   parts sliced into rounds
2 ripe tomatoes, finely chopped

2 Tbsp. finely chopped fresh
   cilantro
¼ tsp. salt, or to taste

CARROT, ONION, AND BELL PEPPER UTHAPPAM

1 green bell pepper, seeded and
   finely chopped
2 carrots, peeled and finely grated

1 red onion, peeled and finely
   chopped
¼ tsp. salt, or to taste

PER VEGETABLE UTHAPPAM:
184 calories, 4g protein, 33g carbohydrates 4g fat, 129mg sodium, omg cholesterol, 1.3g fiber

RAVA DOSAS (FINE CREAM OF WHEAT DOSAS)

*O*ne of the differences between a rava dosa and a masala dosa is the way each is made. The batter in a masala dosa is poured in the center of the skillet, then spread toward the edges; the rava dosa batter is poured from the outer edge of the skillet toward the center in a circular motion. Rava dosas are very thin and crispy, and go well with spicy chutneys.

Prepare the batter half an hour in advance of the cooking.

PREPARATION TIME: *30 minutes* COOKING TIME: *30 minutes* SERVES: *4 (makes 16 dosas)*

1 cup cream of wheat, farina, or fine semolina
1½ cups rice flour or rice powder
½ tsp. salt
2 Tbsp. low-fat plain yogurt
2½ cups water

1 onion, peeled and finely chopped
2 Tbsp. finely chopped fresh cilantro

2–4 green chilies or jalapeño peppers, stemmed and cut into thin rounds
½ tsp. cumin seeds
½ tsp. freshly ground black pepper

¼ cup vegetable oil for the skillet

1. In a mixing bowl, combine the cream of wheat and rice flour. Stir in the salt and yogurt. Add water slowly, to avoid lumps forming in the batter. Set aside for 30 minutes.

2. Add onion, cilantro, green chilies, cumin seeds, and black pepper to the batter and mix.

3. Heat a nonstick skillet over medium heat. Pour a ladleful, or ½ cup, of batter, starting from the outer edge of the skillet, about a half inch from the edge, in a circular motion moving toward the center of the skillet. Add a teaspoon of oil around

the dosa. Cook until golden. Using a spatula, flip the dosa and cook the other side for 1 minute. Serve hot with any coconut chutney (see Chapter 1).

PER RAVA DOSA:
136 calories, 2g protein, 22g carbohydrates, 4.5g fat, 30mg sodium, 0mg cholesterol, 0.8g fiber

---

IDLIS AND SAMBAR

IDLIS (STEAMED RICE AND URAD DAL PATTIES)

*I*dlis are a favorite breakfast food in southern India. Although you must use a special steaming mold, sold in Indian grocery stores, consisting of a central support rod on which several discs or plates are fitted, I am including them because they are not only delicious, but they are such a wonderful part of my mother's cooking. Idlis are round, soft, white fluffy patties, about 3 inches in diameter and eaten with chutney and Sambar (p. 210).

Prepare the batter a day and a half or 36 hours in advance.

PREPARATION TIME: *25 minutes* COOKING TIME: *30 minutes* SERVES: 4 *(makes 16 idlis)*

½ cups urad dal (p. 161)	½ tsp. salt
1 cup long-grain white rice	
½ cup parboiled rice	Vegetable oil spray for the idli
1¾ cups water, divided	mold

1. Pick over and rinse the urad dal, and soak it in a bowl with 5 cups of water for 5 hours. In separate bowls, soak the long-grain rice and the parboiled rice with 5 cups of water each for 4 to 5 hours. Drain the urad dal. In a blender or food processor fitted with a steel blade, process the urad dal with ¾ cup of water until it is smooth and frothy. Pour the dal into a stainless-steel dutch oven or pot with lid, or any container large enough for the batter to rise.

2. Drain the long-grain rice. In a blender or food processor fitted with a steel blade, process the rice with ½ cup of water until very coarse. Add the rice to the pureed dal.

3. Drain the parboiled rice. In a blender or food processor fitted with a steel blade, puree the rice with ½ cup of water until coarse. Add to the dal and rice puree. Add the salt and stir well. Set aside for 36 hours to rise.

4. Before making the idlis, stir the batter well. In a saucepan large enough to hold the idli molds, boil 3 cups of water. Spray the molds with vegetable oil spray and pour ½ cup of batter into each depression. Place the molds in the saucepan, cover, and cook for 10 minutes. Carefully remove the idlis with a large spoon and serve hot with Fresh Coconut and Mint Chutney (page 15) and Sambar (recipe follows).

PER IDLI:

88 calories, 3g protein, 13g carbohydrates, 1g fat, 54mg sodium, omg cholesterol, og fiber

SAMBAR

Sambar is a spicy, souplike dish that is traditionally served with idlis and dosas. Serve it mild, spicy, or extra spicy by adjusting the number of hot peppers in the sambar powder, which is also available in Indian and other Asian grocery stores.

PREPARATION TIME: *20 minutes* COOKING TIME: *1 hour* SERVES: 4–6

½ cup toovar dal or yellow split
   peas
¼ tsp. ground turmeric
3 onions, peeled and thinly sliced
2 ripe tomatoes, thinly sliced
½ cup fresh or thawed frozen peas
1 cup fresh pearl onions, peeled
   and blanched, or thawed frozen
   pearl onions

FOR THE SAMBAR POWDER:
2 tsp. vegetable oil
2–4 dried red chilies, to taste
1 Tbsp. coriander seeds
1½ tsp. cumin seeds
¼ tsp. fenugreek seeds
2 whole cloves
¼ inch cinnamon stick
2 black peppercorns
3 Tbsp. dried coconut powder

FOR THE SEASONING:
2 tsp. vegetable oil
½ tsp. mustard seeds
½ tsp. ground asafetida

1–2 tsp. tamarind paste
1 tsp. brown sugar
1 tsp. salt
1 Tbsp. chopped fresh cilantro

1. Pick over and rinse the toovar dal. In a 3-quart saucepan, boil 5 cups of water. Add the dal and turmeric, and cook over medium-high heat for 40 minutes, until the dal is soft. Set aside.

2. Meanwhile, cook the vegetables. In a saucepan, boil 2 cups of water and add the onions, tomatoes, peas, and pearl onions. Reduce heat to medium and simmer for 15 minutes, until all the vegetables are tender. Drain and set aside.

3. To prepare the sambar powder:
In a small saucepan, heat the oil. Add the red chilies, coriander, cumin, fenugreek, cloves, cinnamon stick, and peppercorns. Roast until the contents of the pan turn a shade darker and you can smell the aroma. Cool for 10 minutes. In a coffee mill or food processor, grind the roasted sambar ingredients and coconut powder to a fine powder. Sambar powder can be stored in a glass jar with a tight-fitting lid for 2 months.

4. To prepare the seasoning:
In the same saucepan, heat the oil. Add the mustard seeds, cover, and lower the heat. When you hear the seeds spatter, add the asafetida and remove from the heat.

5. To the cooked dal, add the vegetables, 1 to 2 teaspoons of the sambar powder, the tamarind paste, brown sugar, salt, and seasoning. If necessary, add water to give the mixture a souplike consistency. Bring to a boil, then lower the heat and simmer for 15 minutes. Garnish with the cilantro and serve hot.

6. You can prepare Sambar two days in advance. Cool, refrigerate, and reheat before serving.

PER SERVING:
88 calories, 3g protein, 10g carbohydrates, 4g fat, 110mg sodium, omg cholesterol, 8g fiber

KANJEEVARAM IDLIS

*K*anjeevaram is a small town in southern India that is known for these spicy idlis made with fresh ginger, black pepper, cilantro, and cashews.

Prepare the batter one day in advance.

PREPARATION TIME: *30 minutes* COOKING TIME: *30 minutes* SERVES: 4 *(makes 16 idlis)*

1 cup urad dal (p. 161)
1 cup long-grain white rice
1¼ cups water
¼ tsp. baking soda
1 tsp. cumin seeds
1 cup low-fat plain yogurt
½ tsp. salt
1 inch fresh ginger, peeled and minced

2 Tbsp. finely chopped fresh cilantro
1 Tbsp. melted ghee or butter
10 cashews, chopped fine
1 tsp. freshly ground black pepper

Vegetable oil spray for the idli molds

1. Rinse the urad dal and rice. Soak the dal and rice in a bowl with 5 cups of water for 3 to 4 hours. Drain the water and, in a blender or food processor fitted with a steel blade, process the rice and dal and 1¼ cups water until the batter is thick and coarse. Put the batter in a dutch oven or a pot with a lid and set aside, covered, to rise in a warm place for a day.

2. Stir the baking soda, cumin, yogurt, salt, ginger, cilantro, ghee, cashews, and pepper into the batter.

3. Spray the idli molds with vegetable oil spray.

4. In a saucepan large enough to hold the molds, boil 2 cups of water. Pour the batter into the molds, place them in the saucepan, cover, and steam for 25 minutes, until the idlis are cooked.

5. Remove the molds from the water and let cool for 2 minutes. Remove the idlis from the molds and serve hot with any chutney (see Chapter 1).

PER IDLI:

106 calories, 5g protein, 17g carbohydrates, 2g fat, 64mg sodium, 3.2mg cholesterol, 0g fiber

RAVA IDLIS

*hese idlis are made out of dry-roasted cream of wheat and yogurt. Prepare the batter half an hour in advance.

PREPARATION TIME: *30 minutes* COOKING TIME: *30 minutes* SERVES: 4

2 cups cream of wheat, farina, or
   fine semolina
2 cups low-fat plain yogurt
2 Tbsp. finely chopped cilantro
2 tsp. salt
½ tsp. baking soda
10–12 cashews, chopped fine

1 carrot, peeled and finely grated
2–8 green chilies or jalapeño
   peppers, finely minced
¼ cup peas, cooked (optional)

Vegetable oil spray for the idli
   molds

1. In a nonstick skillet, dry-roast the cream of wheat for 5 to 6 minutes, until it turns a shade darker. Cool.
2. In a bowl, mix the roasted cream of wheat and yogurt, taking care to avoid lumps. Add the cilantro, salt, baking soda, cashews, carrot, and green chilies (and peas, if desired). Let the batter rest for 5 minutes.
3. Spray the idli molds with vegetable oil spray.
4. In a saucepan large enough to hold the idli molds, boil 3 cups of water. Fill the molds with batter. Put the molds in the saucepan and cook, covered, for 20 minutes, until the idlis are cooked.
5. Remove the molds from the water and let cool for 2 minutes. Remove the idlis from the molds and serve hot with any chutney (see Chapter 1).

PER IDLI:
   95 calories, 4g protein, 15g carbohydrates, 2g fat, 60mg sodium, 2.5mg cholesterol, 1g fiber

CHAPTER 11

SWEET BEVERAGES AND DESSERTS

....

MANGO MILKSHAKE

ALMOND AND PISTACHIO MILK

ALMOND-SAFFRON MILK

SWEET YOGURT DRINK

MINTY YOGURT DRINK

BANANA YOGURT SHAKE

FRESH PAPAYA AND YOGURT DRINK

SPICED TEA

SPICED TEA WITH FRESH MINT AND GINGER

SEMOLINA HALVA WITH GOLDEN RAISINS

CARROT HALVA PUDDING

CREAM PUDDING

MANGOES WITH CREAM

SWEET VERMICELLI PUDDING

RICE PUDDING

TAPIOCA MILK PUDDING

COCONUT FUDGE

ALMOND MILK FUDGE

CASHEW NUT FUDGE

GULAB JAMOONS

SWEET BEVERAGES AND DESSERTS

SWEET BEVERAGES

Since India is a tropical country, beverages are served at any time of the day. Mangoes, bananas, papayas, and other fruits are pureed with milk or yogurt and are enriched by aromatic spices such as cardamom and cinnamon. These drinks add a fancy sweet touch and a special finale to a spicy meal.

·····

MANGO MILKSHAKE

Mangoes are very tasty tropical fruits. If mangoes are not in season, you can substitute canned mango pulp. Canned pulp is usually sweetened, so adjust the sugar in the recipe accordingly. Yogurt or buttermilk can be substituted for the milk.

PREPARATION TIME: *10 minutes* NO COOKING SERVES: 4

> *1 large fresh mango, peeled,*   *3–4 Tbsp. sugar*
> *seeded, and diced, or 1 cup*   *¼ tsp. ground cardamom*
> *canned mango pulp*   *3 cups chilled low-fat or skim milk*

In a blender, combine the mango, sugar, cardamom, and 1 cup of the milk. Blend for 2 to 3 minutes, until pureed. Add the remaining milk and blend for another minute. Serve in a glass over ice.

PER SERVING:
162 calories, 7g protein, 29g carbohydrates, 2g fat, 93mg sodium, 7.5g cholesterol, 1g fiber

ALMOND AND PISTACHIO MILK

*T*he sweet taste of these nuts lends a special flavor to this refreshing drink.

PREPARATION TIME: *20 minutes* COOKING TIME: *25 minutes* SERVES: 4

¼ cup slivered almonds, blanched
¼ cup unsalted pistachios, blanched
*   and chopped*
1 cup boiling water
3 cups 1% milk

3 Tbsp. sugar
⅛ tsp. ground cardamom
2 drops rose essence or 1 Tbsp.
*   rose water (optional)*

In a bowl, soak the almonds and pistachios in the boiling water for 30 minutes. Drain. Place the nuts and 1 cup of the milk in a blender and puree to a fine paste. In a saucepan, combine the puree, the remaining milk, sugar, and cardamom (and rose essence, if desired), and simmer for 20 minutes. Chill. Serve over ice.

PER SERVING:
    201 calories, 9g protein, 21g carbohydrates, 9g fat, 90mg sodium, 7.5mg cholesterol, 1g fiber

ALMOND-SAFFRON MILK

*S*affron threads impart a beautiful orange-yellow color and distinctive flavor and aroma to this refreshing drink.

PREPARATION TIME: *25 minutes* COOKING TIME: *25 minutes* SERVES: 4

½ cup slivered almonds, blanched
1 cup boiling water
3 cups 1% milk

½ tsp. saffron threads
4 Tbsp. sugar or honey
⅛ tsp. ground cardamom

In a bowl, soak the almonds in the boiling water for 30 minutes. Drain. In a blender, puree the almonds and 1 cup of the milk to a fine paste. In a saucepan, combine the paste, the remaining milk, saffron threads, sugar, and cardamom, and simmer over medium heat for 20 minutes, bringing the mixture to a boil. On a cold winter night, serve this drink hot, or in summer, serve cold over ice.

PER SERVING:
   210 calories, 8g protein, 24g carbohydrates, 9g fat, 90mg sodium, 7.5mg cholesterol, 1g fiber

SWEET YOGURT DRINK (SWEET LASSI)

A good-quality yogurt is essential in preparing a tasty lassi. Homemade yogurt (p. 9) from whole milk is best for this drink—it gives the drink a wonderful richness and depth.

PREPARATION TIME: *5 minutes* NO COOKING SERVES: 4

   3 cups fresh, low-fat plain yogurt   1 Tbsp. rose water (optional)
   ½ cup ice water   4 Tbsp. half-and-half (optional)
   4 Tbsp. sugar

In a blender, process the yogurt, ice water, and sugar (and rose water, if desired) until the mixture is frothy. Serve over ice (with a splash of half-and-half in each glass, if desired).

PER SERVING:
   177 calories, 9g protein, 24g carbohydrates, 5g fat, 125mg sodium, 22mg cholesterol, 0g fiber

MINTY YOGURT DRINK

*F*resh mint and ground roasted cumin seeds make this a soothing summer drink.

PREPARATION TIME: *10 minutes* NO COOKING SERVES: 4

2 cups low-fat plain yogurt
1½ cups cold water
12 mint leaves
Salt to taste

1 tsp. dry-roasted cumin seeds,
    coarsely ground
1 Tbsp. finely chopped fresh
    cilantro

In a blender, process 1 cup of the yogurt, the water, and the mint leaves for 1 minute, until the mint is finely chopped. Add the salt, cumin seeds, cilantro, and the remaining yogurt, and process for 1 minute more, until the mixture is frothy. Serve over ice.

PER SERVING:
    111 calories, 9g protein, 12g carbohydrates, 3g fat, 120mg sodium, 10mg cholesterol, 0g fiber

BANANA YOGURT SHAKE

*T*his is light, healthy, and a breeze to prepare. It is a perfect ending to a spicy dinner. You can substitute apples or pineapple for the bananas.

PREPARATION TIME: *10 minutes* NO COOKING SERVES: 4

2 cups low-fat plain yogurt or
    buttermilk
1 cup ice water
2 ripe bananas, peeled and sliced

3 Tbsp. sugar
⅛ tsp. ground cardamom
¼ tsp. freshly ground nutmeg

In a blender, process the yogurt, water, bananas, sugar, and cardamom for 2 to 3 minutes, until the mixture is frothy. Serve over ice with a sprinkle of nutmeg on top.

PER SERVING:
162 calories, 6g protein, 30g carbohydrates, 2g fat, 80mg sodium, 10mg cholesterol, 1g fiber

FRESH PAPAYA AND YOGURT DRINK

Sweet papayas make this a temptingly delicious and soothing ice-cold drink.

PREPARATION TIME: *10 minutes* NO COOKING SERVES: 4

*1 papaya, peeled, seeded, and
    chopped
2 cups low-fat plain yogurt*

*1 cup ice water
1–2 Tbsp. sugar or honey*

In a blender, puree all the ingredients. Serve over ice.

PER SERVING:
126 calories, 6g protein, 21g carbohydrates, 2g fat, 82mg sodium, 10mg cholesterol, 0.5g fiber

SPICED TEA

What a wonderful way to end the day—with a piping-hot cup of tea!

PREPARATION TIME: *5 minutes* COOKING TIME: *15 minutes* SERVES: 4

*2 cups cold water
2 cups 2% milk
5 orange pekoe tea bags or 3 tsp.
    loose tea*

*2 whole cloves
3 green cardamom pods
1 inch cinnamon stick
Sugar to taste*

In a saucepan, combine the water and milk. Bring to a boil. Stir in the tea, cloves, cardamom pods, and cinnamon stick, and simmer for 5 minutes. Turn off the heat and let the tea steep for a couple of minutes. Add the sugar and simmer for 5 minutes. Taste for sugar and milk. Strain the tea and serve immediately.

PER SERVING:
86 calories, 4g protein, 14g carbohydrates, 1.3g fat, 62mg sodium, 10mg cholesterol, 0g fiber

SPICED TEA WITH FRESH MINT AND GINGER

Fresh mint and ginger lend an Indian perk to this tea. If you are out of ginger, don't worry—this tea tastes great just with fresh mint.

PREPARATION TIME: *5 minutes* COOKING TIME: *20 minutes* SERVES: *4*

2 cups 2% milk
2 cups water
5 orange pekoe tea bags or 3 tsp.
   loose tea

3 sprigs fresh mint
Sugar to taste

In a saucepan, combine all the ingredients and bring to a boil. Turn down the heat and simmer on low for 10 minutes. Turn off the heat and let the tea steep for 2 minutes. Taste for milk and sugar, and add more if necessary. Strain the tea and serve immediately.

PER SERVING:
86 calories, 4g protein, 14g carbohydrates, 1.5g fat, 61mg sodium, 10mg cholesterol, 0g fiber

DESSERTS

On a typical day, dessert in our household consists of a piece of fruit, but on special occasions, there is no finer way to end a celebratory meal than to indulge in one of these delicious desserts that follow. Brimming with the rich taste of fruits, cream, butter, and sugar, these desserts are absolutely irresistible. You can enjoy the simple-to-prepare and perfectly refreshing desserts all year long.

SEMOLINA HALVA WITH GOLDEN RAISINS

(KESARIBHAT)

*R*oasted cream of wheat is laced with golden raisins and saffron threads. This quick and easy dessert tastes great served either hot or at room temperature.

PREPARATION TIME: *10 minutes* COOKING TIME: *25 minutes* SERVES: *4*

1 cup fine-grained semolina or farina or instant cream of wheat
½ cup melted ghee or butter
6–8 cashews, chopped
2 Tbsp. golden raisins

2 cups water (or 1 cup water plus 1 cup 2% milk)
¾–1 cup sugar, to taste
¼ tsp. saffron threads
⅛ tsp. ground cardamom

1. In a nonstick skillet, roast the semolina over medium heat for 5 minutes, stirring constantly, until it turns a shade darker. Take off the heat and set aside.

2. In a heavy nonstick saucepan, heat 1 tablespoon of the ghee or butter. Add the cashews and raisins, and sauté over medium-low heat for 1 minute, until the cashews turn light brown and the raisins plump. Add the water, sugar, saffron threads, and cardamom, and bring to the boil. Reduce the heat to low, and stirring constantly, slowly pour the semolina into the saucepan. Keep stirring until all the water is absorbed. Stir in the remaining ghee or butter. Simmer for 2 minutes. Serve hot.

PER SERVING:

590 calories, 6g protein, 85g carbohydrates, 25g fat, 5mg sodium, 65mg cholesterol, 1.5g fiber

CARROT HALVA PUDDING (GAJAR HALVA)

Grated carrots are cooked in milk until they are tender and then reduced to the consistency of pudding. This tastes best when chilled and served with whipped cream.

PREPARATION TIME: *25 minutes* COOKING TIME: *45 minutes* SERVES: 6

2 cups whole milk
4 Tbsp. ghee or unsalted butter,
   melted
8 cashews, chopped
2 Tbsp. golden raisins
1½ lbs. carrots, peeled and finely
   grated

3 Tbsp. sweetened condensed milk
½ cup sugar
⅛ tsp. ground cardamom
⅛ tsp. ground nutmeg

1. In a heavy-bottomed 3-quart saucepan, bring the milk to a boil. Reduce the heat to medium-low and simmer for 20 to 25 minutes, until the milk is reduced by half. In a large nonstick saucepan, heat 1 tablespoon of the ghee. Add the cashews and raisins, and roast until the cashews are golden and the raisins plump. Add the grated carrots and sauté over medium-low heat for 10 minutes, until the carrots are tender.
2. Add the cooked carrots to the saucepan with the reduced milk. Simmer for 15 minutes, until the carrots are cooked, then add the remaining 3 tablespoons of ghee, the condensed milk, sugar, cardamom, and nutmeg, and cook until the milk is absorbed and the mixture has the consistency of pudding. Serve hot or chilled.

PER SERVING:

340 calories, 7g protein, 60g carbohydrates, 8g fat, 133mg sodium, 30mg cholesterol, 5g fiber

CREAM PUDDING (BASOONDI)

Almonds and pistachios provide a crunchy foil to this silky pudding made with an infusion of milk and sugar.

PREPARATION TIME: *5 minutes* COOKING TIME: *1 hour* SERVES: 6

8 cups whole milk
4 Tbsp. sugar or honey
2 Tbsp. unsalted pistachios,
   slivered and blanched

2 Tbsp. almonds, slivered and
   blanched

In a heavy-bottomed nonstick 5-quart pan, bring the milk to a boil. Reduce the heat and simmer for 45 to 50 minutes, stirring frequently with a long spoon, until the milk is reduced by one quarter to approximately 2¼ cups and has the consistency of a thick cream sauce. Add the sugar and nuts. Mix well. Let cool, then refrigerate. Serve chilled.

PER SERVING:
   400 calories, 17g protein, 35g carbohydrates, 21g fat, 240mg sodium, 46mg cholesterol, 0g fiber

MANGOES WITH CREAM

If fresh mangoes aren't in season, you can make this easy, light dessert with canned mangoes.

PREPARATION TIME: *5 minutes* NO COOKING SERVES: 4

1 large ripe mango, peeled and
   seeded

FOR THE TOPPING:
½ cup low-fat sour cream
1 Tbsp. sugar
½ tsp. crushed saffron threads

1. Cut the mango into large pieces. Chill for 30 minutes.
2. Meanwhile, prepare the topping. Combine the sour cream, sugar, and saffron threads in a small bowl. Cover and chill for 30 minutes.
3. Serve the mangoes with the topping.

PER SERVING:
    102 calories, 0.3g protein, 12g carbohydrates, 6g fat, 10mg sodium, 10mg cholesterol, 0.5g fiber

SWEET VERMICELLI PUDDING

This is a light, teatime sweet laced with cashews and raisins.

PREPARATION TIME: *10 minutes* COOKING TIME: *20 minutes* SERVES: 4

8 oz. uncooked vermicelli	1 cup water
1 Tbs. melted ghee or unsalted butter	3 cups 2% milk, boiled
	½ tsp. saffron threads
4 cashews, chopped	½ cup sugar
1 Tbsp. golden raisins or currants	

1. Break the vermicelli into 2-inch pieces.
2. In a 3-quart saucepan, heat the ghee. Add the cashews and raisins, and sauté for 1 minute, until the cashews turn golden and the raisins plump. Stir in the vermicelli and sauté over medium-low heat until the vermicelli is golden. Add the water and simmer for 2 minutes, until the vermicelli is tender.
3. Add the boiled milk and saffron threads, and bring to a boil. Reduce the heat, add the sugar, and simmer for 5 minutes.
4. Serve hot, warm, or chilled.

PER SERVING:
    323 calories, 8g protein, 48g carbohydrates, 11g fat, 120mg sodium, 22mg cholesterol, 1g fiber

RICE PUDDING

❧

*T*his light, luscious pudding is flavored with cardamom and nutmeg, and garnished with almonds and raisins.

PREPARATION TIME: *5 minutes* COOKING TIME: *30 minutes* SERVES: 4

½ cup long-grain white rice
1½ cups water
2 cups whole milk
2 Tbsp. golden raisins
2 Tbsp. almonds, slivered and
   blanched

1 cup sugar
⅛ tsp. ground cardamom
⅛ tsp. ground nutmeg

1. Rinse the rice and drain it. In a saucepan, boil the water and stir in the rice. Cook for 10 minutes, until the rice is half done. Drain.
2. In a 3-quart saucepan, bring the milk to a boil and add the rice. Simmer over medium heat for 20 minutes, stirring occasionally. When the rice is soft and the milk begins to thicken, stir in the raisins, almonds, sugar, cardamom, and nutmeg, and stir constantly for 5 minutes.
3. Serve warm or chilled.

PER SERVING:
   366 calories, 6g protein, 72g carbohydrates, 7g fat, 60mg sodium, 17mg cholesterol, 0.5g fiber

TAPIOCA MILK PUDDING

❧

*T*his recipe makes a rich, creamy, not-too-sweet pudding with a touch of nutmeg flavor.

PREPARATION TIME: *5 minutes* COOKING TIME: *25 minutes* SERVES: 4

2 cups water
1 cup uncooked tapioca
1 Tbsp. melted ghee or unsalted
    butter
2 Tbsp. golden raisins
1 Tbsp. chopped cashews

2 cups whole milk
½ cup sugar
⅛ tsp. ground cardamom
⅛ tsp. ground nutmeg
2 Tbsp. unsalted pistachios,
    blanched and chopped

1. In a saucepan, boil the water. Add the tapioca and simmer over medium heat about 15 minutes, until the tapioca is tender and translucent.

2. In a small sauté pan, heat the ghee. Add the raisins and cashews, and sauté until the cashews turn golden and the raisins plump. Remove them from the pan with a slotted spoon and drain on paper towels.

3. In a 3-quart saucepan, heat the milk. Add the sugar, cardamom, nutmeg, raisins, cashews, and the tapioca, and simmer over low heat for 5 minutes.

4. Serve hot, warm, or chilled, sprinkled with pistachios.

PER SERVING:

395 calories, 6g protein, 68g carbohydrates, 11g fat, 98mg sodium, 26mg cholesterol, 0.5g fiber

COCONUT FUDGE (NARIAL BARFI)

This elegant, rich dessert is filled with the intense flavor of coconut. Use only freshly grated coconut for this fudge.

PREPARATION TIME: 20 minutes COOKING TIME: 35 minutes SERVES: 4–6

2 Tbsp. melted ghee or unsalted
    butter
1 Tbsp. unsalted cashews, roasted
    and chopped
1 Tbsp. golden raisins

1 cup freshly grated coconut
1 cup sugar
½ cup water
⅛ tsp. ground cardamom

1. Grease a 9-inch-square baking dish or pan. Set aside.
2. In a small saucepan, heat the ghee. Add the cashews and raisins, and cook until the cashews are golden and the raisins plump. Set aside.
3. Heat a large heavy-bottomed nonstick pan. Add the grated coconut and sauté over medium heat, stirring constantly, for 5 minutes, until the coconut loses its moisture and looks flaky. Remove from the pan and set aside.
4. Using the same pan, combine the sugar and ½ cup of water, and bring to a boil over medium heat. Cook for 8 to 10 minutes, until the mixture is thickened and looks frothy and bubbly. Add the grated coconut, cashews, raisins, and cardamom, and cook for 10 minutes, stirring vigorously, until the coconut mixture begins to foam.
5. Immediately pour the mixture into the greased baking dish. Spread the mixture with a flat spatula to form an even layer. Let it cool for 5 minutes. Cut into 1-inch pieces. Serve.
6. This fudge stays fresh for 2 weeks stored in airtight containers.

PER SERVING (2 PIECES):
177 calories, 0.5g protein, 28g carbohydrates, 7g fat, 32mg sodium, 8mg cholesterol, 1.5g fiber

ALMOND MILK FUDGE (BADAM BARFI)

*S*weet-tasting almonds are blended in milk to make this rich, delicious fudge.

PREPARATION TIME: *15 minutes* COOKING TIME: *40 minutes* SERVES: *4–6* (makes 14 pieces)

1 cup blanched almonds	*⅓ cup sugar*
(approximately ½ lb.)	*1 Tbsp. melted ghee or unsalted*
1 cup whole milk	*butter*

1. In a coffee grinder or food processor fitted with a steel blade, grind the almonds to a fine powder. Set aside.

2. Grease an 8-inch-square pan, a cookie sheet, or a sheet of wax paper.

3. In a heavy-bottomed nonstick pan, bring the milk to a boil. Turn down the heat and cook on medium-high for 20 minutes, stirring constantly, until the milk thickens and has the consistency of cream soup.

4. Add the sugar and reduce the heat to medium. Cook until the sugar is dissolved. Add the ghee and the powdered almonds. Stir vigorously with a wooden spoon until the mixture begins to harden and sticks to the spoon. Stir for a couple of more minutes, then pour the mixture onto the greased pan or wax paper.

5. With a spatula, quickly spread the mixture evenly. While the fudge is still hot, dip a knife into cold water and cut the fudge into diamond-shaped pieces. Serve.

6. Stored in the refrigerator, this fudge keeps for 2 weeks.

PER SERVING (2 PIECES):
178 calories, 4.5g protein, 13g carbohydrates, 12g fat, 30mg sodium, 6mg cholesterol, 1.2g fiber

CASHEW NUT FUDGE (KAJOO BARFI)

ashews are soaked and ground to a fine paste, then cooked with sugar to a thick, rich consistency.

PREPARATION TIME: *1 hour* COOKING TIME: *45 minutes* SERVES: *4–6 (makes 12 pieces)*

> *1 cup raw, unsalted cashews*
> *1 cup whole milk*
> *⅓ cup sugar*
> *1 Tbsp. melted ghee or unsalted*
> *butter*

1. Soak the cashews in boiling water for 1 hour. Drain.

2. In a blender or food processor fitted with a steel blade, process the cashews and whole milk to a fine puree. Set aside.

3. Grease a 9-inch-square baking pan or a cookie sheet.

4. In a heavy-bottomed nonstick sauté pan, combine the nut paste and the sugar. Cook over medium heat for 5 minutes. Reduce the heat to medium-low and cook, stirring constantly, scraping down the sides now and then, for 20 minutes, until the fudge thickens. Add the ghee and cook for 1 minute longer.

5. Pour the fudge onto the greased pan, spreading it evenly. Let it cool. Dip a knife into cold water and cut the fudge into 1½-inch diamond-shaped pieces. Serve.

6. Stored in the refrigerator, this fudge keeps for 2 to 3 weeks.

PER SERVING (2 PIECES):
    168 calories, 3.5g protein, 15g carbohydrates, 10g fat, 32mg sodium, 6mg cholesterol, 0.5g fiber

GULAB JAMOONS

A light pastry made from dry milk and Bisquick mix is deep-fried and soaked in a light, sugary syrup. It is an all-time favorite among our family and friends.

PREPARATION TIME: 20 *minutes*   COOKING TIME: 45 *minutes*   SERVES: 4–6 *(makes 24 jamoons)*

FOR THE SYRUP:
4 cups water
3 cups sugar

FOR THE JAMOONS:
1 cup nonfat dry milk powder
1 cup Bisquick baking mix
⅓ cup 2% milk

1 tbsp. soft ghee or sweet butter
Vegetable oil for deep-frying

1. To prepare the syrup:
In a saucepan, bring the water and sugar to a boil. Turn down the heat and simmer over medium until the sugar dissolves. Set aside.

2. To prepare the jamoons:
In a bowl, mix the milk powder and Bisquick, and slowly stir in the milk until the mixture forms a soft dough. Let rest for 10 minutes.

3. In the bowl, knead the dough for a couple of minutes. Dab a little ghee on the palm of your hand. Take a small piece of dough and roll it in your palm, making a ½-inch smooth round ball. Set aside covered with a damp cloth. Repeat the process with the remaining dough, applying more ghee now and then on your palm.

4. In a deep-frying pan, heat the vegetable oil over medium heat. The oil is ready when the temperature reaches 250 degrees, or when a small piece of dough dropped into the pan rises slowly to the top. Carefully, drop ten to twelve dough balls into the pan. Maintain the oil temperature at 250 degrees throughout. After a minute, the dough should double in size. Keep stirring over low heat until the balls turn a golden brown. With a slotted spoon, remove them and drain them on paper towels. Repeat with the remaining dough.

5. As they are drained, drop the balls into the lukewarm sugar syrup. Set aside for 1 hour. Serve.

PER SERVING (2 JAMOONS):
252 calories, 1.5g protein, 57g carbohydrates, 2.5g fat, 137mg sodium, 3mg cholesterol, 1g fiber

INDEX

About the Author

VASANTHA PRASAD was born in Bangalore, India, and developed a passion for vegetarian cooking in her late teens. Living in a country renowned for its exotic spices and wide variety of vegetables, not to mention age-old family culinary secrets, she learned to prepare healthful and tasty vegetarian delights.

She received a B.A. in economics, political science, and sociology. She has been happily married for thirty years to Balasa Prasad, a physician, and has one daughter, Bindu. She works as a full-time office manager in her husband's office. Her hobbies are cooking, reading, and gardening—she grows several herbs and vegetables in her own garden.

When she came to the United States in 1972, she was surprised to see that there were so few vegetarians. Since then she has had a dream of writing a cookbook with recipes that skillfully blend the enticing flavors of the East with the quick and practical methods of the West. This is her first cookbook.

ABOUT THE TYPE

The text of this book was set in Sabon, a typeface designed by the well-known German typographer Jan Tschichold (1902–74). Sabon's design is based upon the original letterforms of Claude Garamond and was created specifically to be used for three sources: foundry type for hand composition, Linotype, and Monotype. Tschichold named his typeface for the famous Frankfurt typefounder Jacques Sabon, who died in 1580.

Printed in the United States
by Baker & Taylor Publisher Services